∼ GREATEST ∼
LOVE POEMS

∼ GREATEST ∼
LOVE POEMS

A comprehensive anthology
of the world's finest romantic verse

Edited by
Madeleine Edgar

ARCTURUS

ARCTURUS

This edition published in 2010 by Arcturus Publishing Limited
26/27 Bickels Yard, 151–153 Bermondsey Street,
London SE1 3HA

Created for Arcturus Publishing by Omnipress Ltd,
Eastbourne, Sussex.

ISBN: 978-1-84837-480-5
AD000070EN

Printed in China

Contents

Introduction

Love. It raises us to the heights of joy. It lowers us to the depths of despair. It makes the world go round and, according to John Lennon, it is all you need.

Of all the emotions, love is perhaps the strongest. For love people have killed, gone to war, cheated and lied, blinded by passion, normal behaviour in suspension. For love, or the lack of it, people have taken their own lives or retreated into solitude, dispensing with the world and its false hopes. The ability to love is one of life's driving forces and one of the principal attributes that makes us human, separating us from the animal world.

Of course, there are many kinds of love – love of country, love of God, love of family or love, even, of a particular place. However, it is the love of another person that has most distracted our poets over the centuries since Geoffrey Chaucer began to write about the human comedy in a language that could be understood by all. The sheer volume of love poems written since is certain proof of the power of this maverick emotion and its effect upon the senses. And rarely can the creation of a piece of artistic endeavour be as intense as that experienced by the poet writing about the object of his or her love. The depth of feeling expressed by John Donne, writing four hundred years ago in *The Good Morrow*, is as powerful and immediate now as it was then:

And now good-morrow to our waking souls,
Which watch not one another out of fear
For love, all love of other sights controls,
And makes one little room an everywhere.

A couple of centuries later, Elizabeth Barrett Browning relived that intensity in her *Sonnets from the Portuguese*, written in the year between first meeting and marrying Robert Browning. Perhaps these could be said to be amongst the greatest lines in the history of the love poem:

How do I love thee? Let me count the ways.
I love thee to the depth and breadth and height
My soul can reach, when feeling out of sight
For the ends of Being and ideal Grace.

These are lines with which all who have loved can identify. They remind us of the impossibility of defining love, because by defining it we limit it and as the poet writes, the scope of her love is as limitless as the scope of her soul, her very being.

Of course, the path of true love rarely runs smoothly and this collection attempts to encompass the entire arc of love. There are poems of romantic longing for a loved one; poems of the love that endures distance after a reluctant parting; poems of the love that is tragically not returned; poems of the love that binds two people together for life in marriage and poems that express

the devastation of a lost love, as so poignantly expressed in
Byron's lines in *So We'll Go No More A-Roving*:

So we'll go no more a-roving
So late into the night,
Though the heart be still as loving,
And the moon be still as bright

For the sword outwears its sheath,
And the soul wears out the breast,
And the heart must pause to breathe,
And love itself have rest.

If you have experienced the heartbreak of a broken romance
– and who has not? – these lines will provide comfort as will
many of the other poems in the Lost Love section of this book,
poems such as John Clare's *Love's Pains* or Robert Burns' *The
Banks o' Doon*. The other sections will accompany you through
other types of romantic sentiments, good and bad. Christina
Rossetti's *Remember* and Hart Crane's *Carrier Letter* are just a
couple of poems in this collection that will provide solace when
you are parted from your loved one. Rossetti writes longingly:

Remember me when I am gone away,
Gone far away into the silent land;
When you can no more hold me by the hand,
Nor I half turn to go, yet turning stay.

And if you attain what is arguably the pinnacle of love's striving, the act of marriage itself, there are many poems in the Poems for Marriage section that will provide the appropriate words to enhance that celebration, such as those of the 17th-century American poet, Anne Bradstreet, in her work *To My Dear and Loving Husband*:

I prize thy love more than whole Mines of gold,
Or all the riches that the East doth hold.
My love is such that Rivers cannot quench,
Nor aught but love from thee give recompense.

Ultimately love is many things – pain, joy, suffering, release, exultation, desperation. Above all, however, it is an exhilarating experience, a transcendent feeling that every human being should live through just once. Perhaps it is up to the master of the English language and the doyen of the love poem, as well as much else, William Shakespeare, to enjoy the last, romantic word:

Shall I compare thee to a summer's day?
Thou art more lovely and more temperate:
Rough winds do shake the darling buds of May,
And summer's lease hath all too short a date.

Romance

Seen through the lens of romance, the object of our love is often idealized, attractions exaggerated and bad points ignored, for love is, after all, blind. Romance has inspired some of the greatest verse in the English language, poems such as Elizabeth Barrett Browning's beautiful sonnet, *How Do I Love Thee?*, the very embodiment of romantic sentiment.

Now Sleeps the Crimson Petal

Now sleeps the crimson petal, now the white;
Nor waves the cypress in the palace walk;
Nor winks the gold fin in the porphyry font:
The firefly wakens: waken thou with me.

Now droops the milkwhite peacock like a ghost,
And like a ghost she glimmers on to me.

Now lies the Earth all Danae to the stars,
And all thy heart lies open unto me.

Now slides the silent meteor on, and leaves
A shining furrow, as thy thoughts in me.

Now folds the lily all her sweetness up,
And slips into the bosom of the lake:
So fold thyself, my dearest, thou, and slip
Into my bosom and be lost in me.

ALFRED, LORD TENNYSON

The Dream

From *A Voyage to the Isle of Love*

All trembling in my arms Aminta lay,
Defending of the bliss I strove to take;
Raising my rapture by her kind delay,
Her force so charming was and weak.
The soft resistance did betray the grant,
While I pressed on the heaven of my desires;
Her rising breasts with nimbler motions pant;
Her dying eyes assume new fires.
Now to the height of languishment she grows,
And still her looks new charms put on;
– Now the last mystery of Love she knows,
We sigh, and kiss: I waked, and all was done.

'Twas but a dream, yet by my heart I knew,
Which still was panting, part of it was true:
Oh how I strove the rest to have believed;
Ashamed and angry to be undeceived!

APHRA BEHN

The Face That Launch'd a Thousand Ships

From *Doctor Faustus*

Was this the face that launch'd a thousand ships,
And burnt the topless towers of Ilium?
Sweet Helen, make me immortal with a kiss.
Her lips suck forth my soul: see, where it flies!
Come, Helen, come, give me my soul again.
Here will I dwell, for heaven is in these lips,
And all is dross that is not Helena.
I will be Paris, and for love of thee,
Instead of Troy, shall Wittenberg be sack'd;
And I will combat with weak Menelaus,
And wear thy colours on my plumed crest;
Yea, I will wound Achilles in the heel,
And then return to Helen for a kiss.
O, thou art fairer than the evening air
Clad in the beauty of a thousand stars;
Brighter art thou than flaming Jupiter
When he appear'd to hapless Semele;
More lovely than the monarch of the sky
In wanton Arethusa's azur'd arms;
And none but thou shalt be my paramour!

CHRISTOPHER MARLOWE

She Walks in Beauty

She walks in beauty, like the night
Of cloudless climes and starry skies,
And all that's best of dark and bright
Meets in her aspect and her eyes;
Thus mellow'd to that tender light
Which Heaven to gaudy day denies.

One shade the more, one ray the less,
Had half impair'd the nameless grace
Which waves in every raven tress
Or softly lightens o'er her face,
Where thoughts serenely sweet express
How pure, how dear their dwelling-place.

And on that cheek and o'er that brow
So soft, so calm, yet eloquent,
The smiles that win, the tints that glow,
But tell of days in goodness spent, –
A mind at peace with all below,
A heart whose love is innocent.

GEORGE GORDON, LORD BYRON

Wild Nights! Wild Nights!

Wild nights! Wild nights!
Were I with thee,
Wild nights should be
Our luxury!

Futile the winds
To a heart in port,
Done with the compass,
Done with the chart.

Rowing in Eden!
Ah! the sea!
Might I but moor
To-night in thee!

EMILY DICKINSON

Love My Love in the Morning

I love my love in the morning,
For she like morn is fair –
Her blushing cheek, its crimson streak,

Its clouds her golden hair.
Her glance, its beam, so soft and kind;
Her tears, its dewy showers;
And her voice, the tender whispering wind
That stirs the early bowers.
I love my love in the morning,
I love my love at noon,
For she is bright as the lord of light,
Yet mild as autumn's moon;
Her beauty is my bosom's sun,
Her faith my fostering shade,
And I will love my darling one,
Till even the sun shall fade.

I love my love in the morning,
I love my love at eve;
Her smile's soft play is like the ray
That lights the western heaven;
I loved her when the sun was high,
I loved her when she rose;
But best of all when evening's sigh
Was murmuring at its close.

GERALD GRIFFIN

Sonnet LXXV

So are you to my thoughts as food to life,
Or as sweet-season'd showers are to the ground;
And for the peace of you I hold such strife
As 'twixt a miser and his wealth is found;
Now proud as an enjoyer and anon
Doubting the filching age will steal his treasure,
Now counting best to be with you alone,
Then better'd that the world may see my pleasure;
Sometime all full with feasting on your sight
And by and by clean starved for a look;
Possessing or pursuing no delight,
Save what is had or must from you be took.
Thus do I pine and surfeit day by day,
Or gluttoning on all, or all away.

WILLIAM SHAKESPEARE

My Lady Looks So Gentle and So Pure

My lady looks so gentle and so pure
When yielding salutation by the way,
That the tongue trembles and has naught to say,
And the eyes, which fain would see, may not endure.
And still, amid the praise she hears secure
She walks with humbleness for her array;
Seeming a creature sent from Heaven to stay
On earth, and show a miracle made sure.
She is so pleasant in the eyes of men
That through the sight the inmost heart doth gain
A sweetness which needs proof to know it by:
And from between her lips there seems to move
A soothing essence that is full of love,
Saying for ever to the spirit, 'Sigh!'

DANTE ALIGHIERI

To His Coy Mistress

Had we but world enough, and time,
This coyness, lady, were no crime.
We would sit down and think which way
To walk, and pass our long love's day;
Thou by the Indian Ganges' side
Shouldst rubies find; I by the tide
Of Humber would complain. I would
Love you ten years before the Flood;
And you should, if you please, refuse
Till the conversion of the Jews.
My vegetable love should grow
Vaster than empires, and more slow.
An hundred years should go to praise
Thine eyes, and on thy forehead gaze;
Two hundred to adore each breast,
But thirty thousand to the rest;
An age at least to every part,
And the last age should show your heart.
For, lady, you deserve this state,
Nor would I love at lower rate.

But at my back I always hear
Time's winged chariot hurrying near;
And yonder all before us lie

Deserts of vast eternity.
Thy beauty shall no more be found,
Nor, in thy marble vault, shall sound
My echoing song; then worms shall try
That long preserv'd virginity,
And your quaint honour turn to dust,
And into ashes all my lust.
The grave's a fine and private place,
But none I think do there embrace.

Now therefore, while the youthful hue
Sits on thy skin like morning dew,
And while thy willing soul transpires
At every pore with instant fires,
Now let us sport us while we may;
And now, like am'rous birds of prey,
Rather at once our time devour,
Than languish in his slow-chapp'd power.
Let us roll all our strength, and all
Our sweetness, up into one ball;
And tear our pleasures with rough strife
Thorough the iron gates of life.
Thus, though we cannot make our sun
Stand still, yet we will make him run.

ANDREW MARVELL

I Love Thee

I love thee, as I love the calm
Of sweet, star-lighted hours!
I love thee, as I love the balm
Of early jes'mine flow'rs.

I love thee, as I love the last
Rich smile of fading day,
Which lingereth, like the look we cast,
On rapture pass'd away.

I love thee as I love the tone
Of some soft-breathing flute
Whose soul is wak'd for me alone,
When all beside is mute.

I love thee as I love the first
Young violet of the spring;
Or the pale lily, April-nurs'd,
To scented blossoming.

I love thee, as I love the full,
Clear gushings of the song,

Which lonely – sad – and beautiful –
At night-fall floats along,

Pour'd by the bul-bul forth to greet
The hours of rest and dew;
When melody and moonlight meet
To blend their charm, and hue.

I love thee, as the glad bird loves
The freedom of its wing,
On which delightedly it moves
In wildest wandering.

I love thee as I love the swell,
And hush, of some low strain,
Which bringeth, by its gentle spell,
The past to life again.

Such is the feeling which from thee
Nought earthly can allure:
'Tis ever link'd to all I see
Of gifted – high – and pure!

ELIZA ACTON

Love's Trinity

Soul, heart, and body, we thus singly name,
Are not in love divisible and distinct,
But each with each inseparably link'd.
One is not honour, and the other shame,
But burn as closely fused as fuel, heat and flame.

They do not love who give the body and keep
The heart ungiven; nor they who yield the soul,
And guard the body. Love doth give the whole;
Its range being high as heaven, as ocean deep,
Wide as the realms of air or planet's curving sweep.

ALFRED AUSTIN

Let's Live and Love: to Lesbia

Let us live, my Lesbia, let us love,
and all the words of the old, and so moral,
may they be worth less than nothing to us!
Suns may set, and suns may rise again:
but when our brief light has set,
night is one long everlasting sleep.

Give me a thousand kisses, a hundred more,
another thousand, and another hundred,
and, when we've counted up the many thousands,
confuse them so as not to know them all,
so that no enemy may cast an evil eye,
by knowing that there were so many kisses.

GAIUS VALERIUS CATULLUS

She Comes Not When Noon is on the Roses

She comes not when Noon is on the roses –
Too bright is Day.
She comes not to the Soul till it reposes
From work and play.

But when Night is on the hills, and the great Voices
Roll in from Sea,
By starlight and by candlelight and dreamlight
She comes to me.

HERBERT TRENCH

Madonna of the Evening Flowers

All day long I have been working
Now I am tired.
I call: 'Where are you?'
But there is only the oak tree rustling in the wind.
The house is very quiet,
The sun shines in on your books,
On your scissors and thimble just put down,
But you are not there.
Suddenly I am lonely:
Where are you?
I go about searching.

Then I see you,
Standing under a spire of pale blue larkspur,
With a basket of roses on your arm.
You are cool, like silver,
And you smile.
I think the Canterbury bells are playing little tunes,
You tell me that the peonies need spraying,
That the columbines have overrun all bounds,
That the pyrus japonica should be cut back and rounded.
You tell me these things.
But I look at you, heart of silver,
White heart-flame of polished silver,

Burning beneath the blue steeples of the larkspur,
And I long to kneel instantly at your feet,
While all about us peal the loud, sweet Te Deums of the
Canterbury bells.

AMY LOWELL

Love Not Me

Love not me for comely grace,
For my pleasing eye or face,

Nor for any outward part:
No, nor for a constant heart!
For these may fail or turn to ill:
Should thou and I sever.

Keep, therefore, a true woman's eye,
And love me still, but know not why!
So hast thou the same reason still
To dote upon me ever.

JOHN WILBYE

Sonnet XVIII

Shall I compare thee to a summer's day?
Thou art more lovely and more temperate.
Rough winds do shake the darling buds of May,
And summer's lease hath all too short a date.
Sometime too hot the eye of heaven shines,
And often is his gold complexion dimm'd;
And every fair from fair sometime declines,
By chance or nature's changing course untrimm'd;
But thy eternal summer shall not fade
Nor lose possession of that fair thou ow'st;
Nor shall Death brag thou wander'st in his shade,
When in eternal lines to time thou grow'st:
So long as men can breathe or eyes can see,
So long lives this, and this gives life to thee.

WILLIAM SHAKESPEARE

On the Balcony

In front of the sombre mountains, a faint,
lost ribbon of rainbows;
And between us and it, the thunder;
And down below in the green wheat, the labourers
Stand like dark stumps, still in the green wheat

You are near to me, and your naked
feet in their sandals,
And through the scent of the balcony's naked timber
I distinguish the scent of your hair: so now the limber
Lightning falls from heaven.

Adown the pale-green glacier river floats
A dark boat through the gloom – and whither?
The thunder roars. But still we have each other!
And disappear – what have we but each other?
The boat has gone.

D. H. LAWRENCE

The Flea

Mark but this flea, and mark in this,
How little that which thou deniest me is;
It suck'd me first, and now sucks thee,
And in this flea our two bloods mingled be.
Thou know'st that this cannot be said
A sin, nor shame, nor loss of maidenhead;
Yet this enjoys before it woo,
And pamper'd swells with one blood made of two;
And this, alas! is more than we would do.

O stay, three lives in one flea spare,
Where we almost, yea, more than married are.
This flea is you and I, and this
Our marriage bed, and marriage temple is.
Though parents grudge, and you, we're met,
And cloister'd in these living walls of jet.
Though use make you apt to kill me,
Let not to that self-murder added be,
And sacrilege, three sins in killing three.

Cruel and sudden, hast thou since
Purpled thy nail in blood of innocence?
Wherein could this flea guilty be,
Except in that drop which it suck'd from thee?
Yet thou triumph'st, and say'st that thou
Find'st not thyself nor me the weaker now.

'Tis true; then learn how false fears be;
Just so much honour, when thou yield'st to me,
Will waste, as this flea's death took life from thee.

JOHN DONNE

When I Have Fears

When I have fears that I may cease to be
Before my pen has glean'd my teeming brain,
Before high-piled books, in charactery,
Hold like rich garners the full ripen'd grain;
When I behold, upon the night's starr'd face,
Huge cloudy symbols of a high romance,
And think that I may never live to trace
Their shadows, with the magic hand of chance;
And when I feel, fair creature of an hour,
That I shall never look upon thee more,
Never have relish in the faery power
Of unreflecting love; – then on the shore
Of the wide world I stand alone, and think
Till love and fame to nothingness do sink.

JOHN KEATS

At Last

At last, when all the summer shine
That warmed life's early hours is past,
Your loving fingers seek for mine
And hold them close – at last – at last!
Not oft the robin comes to build
Its nest upon the leafless bough
By autumn robbed, by winter chilled, –
But you, dear heart, you love me now.

Though there are shadows on my brow
And furrows on my cheek, in truth, –
The marks where Time's remorseless plough
Broke up the blooming sward of Youth, –
Though fled is every girlish grace
Might win or hold a lover's vow,
Despite my sad and faded face,
And darkened heart, you love me now!

I count no more my wasted tears;
They left no echo of their fall;
I mourn no more my lonesome years;
This blessed hour atones for all.
I fear not all that Time or Fate
May bring to burden heart or brow, –

Strong in the love that came so late,
Our souls shall keep it always now!

ELIZABETH AKERS ALLEN

On a Girdle

That which her slender waist confined,
　Shall now my joyful temples bind;
No monarch but would give his crown,
His arms might do what this has done.

It was my heaven's extremest sphere,
The pale which held that lovely deer;
My joy, my grief, my hope, my love,
　Did all within this circle move!

A narrow compass! and yet there
Dwelt all that's good, and all that's fair!
Give me but what this riband bound,
Take all the rest the sun goes around!

EDMUND WALLER

Amoretti
Sonnet LXXV

One day I wrote her name upon the strand,
But came the waves and washed it away:
Agayne I wrote it with a second hand,
But came the tyde, and made my paynes his pray.
Vayne men, sayd she, that doest in vaine assay,
A mortall thing so to immortalize,
For I my selve shall lyke to this decay,
And eek my name bee wyped out lykewize.
Not so, (quod I) let baser things devize
To dy in dust, but you shall live by fame:
My verse your vertues rare shall eternize,
And in the hevens wryte your glorious name.
Where whenas death shall al the world subdew,
Our love shall live, and later life renew.

EDMUND SPENSER

The Evening Star

Lo! in the painted oriel of the West,
Whose panes the sunken sun incarnadines,
Like a fair lady at her casement, shines
The evening star, the star of love and rest!
And then anon she doth herself divest
Of all her radiant garments, and reclines
Behind the sombre screen of yonder pines,
With slumber and soft dreams of love oppressed.
O my beloved, my sweet Hesperus!
My morning and my evening star of love!
My best and gentlest lady! even thus,
As that fair planet in the sky above,
Dost thou retire unto thy rest at night,
And from thy darkened window fades the light.

HENRY WADSWORTH LONGFELLOW

Bright Star, Would I Were Stedfast

Bright star, would I were stedfast as thou art –
Not in lone splendour hung aloft the night
And watching, with eternal lids apart,
Like nature's patient, sleepless Eremite,
The moving waters at their priestlike task
Of pure ablution round earth's human shores,
Or gazing on the new soft-fallen mask
Of snow upon the mountains and the moors –
No – yet still stedfast, still unchangeable,
Pillowed upon my fair love's ripening breast,
To feel for ever its soft fall and swell,
Awake for ever in a sweet unrest,
Still, still to hear her tender-taken breath,
And so live ever – or else swoon to death.

JOHN KEATS

Delight in Disorder

A sweet disorder in the dress
Kindles in clothes a wantonness:
A lawn about the shoulders thrown
Into a fine distraction:
An erring lace which here and there
Enthrals the crimson stomacher:
A cuff neglectful, and thereby
Ribbons to flow confusedly:
A winning wave (deserving note)
In the tempestuous petticoat:
A careless shoe-string, in whose tie
I see a wild civility:
Do more bewitch me than when art
Is too precise in every part.

ROBERT HERRICK

Song [Secret Love]

I hid my love when young till I
Couldn't bear the buzzing of a fly;
I hid my love to my despite
Till I could not bear to look at light:
I dare not gaze upon her face
But left her memory in each place;
Where're I saw a wild flower lie
I kissed and bade my love goodbye.

I met her in the greenest dells,
Where dew drops pearl the wood bluebells;
The lost breeze kissed her bright blue eye,
The bee kissed and went singing by,
A sunbeam found a passage there,
A gold chain round her neck so fair;
As secret as the wild bee's song
She lay there all the summer long.

I hid my love in field and town
Till e'en the breeze would knock me down;
The bees seemed singing ballads o'er
The fly's bass turned a lion's roar;
And even silence found a tongue,

To haunt me all the summer long;
The riddle nature could not prove
Was nothing else but secret love.

JOHN CLARE

Meeting at Night

The grey sea and the long black land;
And the yellow half-moon large and low;
And the startled little waves that leap
In fiery ringlets from their sleep,
As I gain the cove with pushing prow,
And quench its speed i' the slushy sand.

Then a mile of warm sea-scented beach;
Three fields to cross till a farm appears;
A tap at the pane, the quick sharp scratch
And blue spurt of a lighted match,
And a voice less loud, thro' its joys and fears,
Than the two hearts beating each to each!

ROBERT BROWNING

Longing

Come to me in my dreams, and then
By day I shall be well again!
For so the night will more than pay
The hopeless longing of the day.

Come, as thou cam'st a thousand times,
A messenger from radiant climes,
And smile on thy new world, and be
As kind to others as to me!

Or, as thou never cam'st in sooth,
Come now, and let me dream it truth,
And part my hair, and kiss my brow,
And say, My love why sufferest thou?

Come to me in my dreams, and then
By day I shall be well again!
For so the night will more than pay
The hopeless longing of the day.

MATTHEW ARNOLD

How Sweet I Roam'd From Field to Field

How sweet I roam'd from field to field,
And tasted all the summer's pride,
'Till I the prince of love beheld,
Who in the sunny beams did glide!

He shew'd me lilies for my hair,
And blushing roses for my brow;
He led me through his gardens fair,
Where all his golden pleasures grow.

With sweet May dews my wings were wet,
And Phoebus fir'd my vocal rage;
He caught me in his silken net,
And shut me in his golden cage.

He loves to sit and hear me sing,
Then, laughing, sports and plays with me;
Then stretches out my golden wing,
And mocks my loss of liberty.

WILLIAM BLAKE

To Jane: The Keen Stars Were Twinkling

The keen stars were twinkling,
And the fair moon was rising among them,
Dear Jane!
The guitar was tinkling,
But the notes were not sweet till you sung them
Again.

As the moon's soft splendour
O'er the faint cold starlight of Heaven
Is thrown,
So your voice most tender
To the strings without soul had then given
Its own.

The stars will awaken,
Though the moon sleep a full hour later,
To-night;
No leaf will be shaken
Whilst the dews of your melody scatter
Delight.

Though the sound overpowers,
Sing again, with your dear voice revealing
A tone
Of some world far from ours,
Where music and moonlight and feeling
Are one.

PERCY BYSSHE SHELLEY

Jenny Kissed Me

Jenny kiss'd me when we met,
Jumping from the chair she sat in;
Time, you thief, who love to get
Sweets into your list, put that in!
Say I'm weary, say I'm sad,
Say that health and wealth have miss'd me,
Say I'm growing old, but add,
Jenny kiss'd me.

JAMES LEIGH HUNT

Love

Love is a breach in the walls, a broken gate,
Where that comes in that shall not go again;
Love sells the proud heart's citadel to Fate.
They have known shame, who love unloved. Even then,
When two mouths, thirsty each for each, find slaking,
And agony's forgot, and hushed the crying
Of credulous hearts, in heaven – such are but taking
Their own poor dreams within their arms, and lying
Each in his lonely night, each with a ghost.
Some share that night. But they know love grows colder,
Grows false and dull, that was sweet lies at most.
Astonishment is no more in hand or shoulder,
But darkens, and dies out from kiss to kiss.
All this is love; and all love is but this.

RUPERT BROOKE

An Evening Song

Look off, dear Love, across the sallow sands,
And mark yon meeting of the sun and sea,
How long they kiss in sight of all the lands.
Ah! longer, longer, we.

Now in the sea's red vintage melts the sun,
As Egypt's pearl dissolved in rosy wine,
And Cleopatra night drinks all. 'Tis done,
Love, lay thine hand in mine.

Come forth, sweet stars, and comfort heaven's heart;
Glimmer, ye waves, round else unlighted sands.
O night! divorce our sun and sky apart
Never our lips, our hands.

SIDNEY LANIER

Dear, I to Thee This Diamond Commend

Dear, I to thee this diamond commend,
In which a model of thyself I send.
How just unto thy joints this circlet sitteth,
So just thy face and shape my fancy fitteth.
The touch will try this ring of purest gold,
My touch tries thee, as pure though softer mold.
That metal precious is, the stone is true,
As true, and then how much more precious you.
The gem is clear, and hath nor needs no foil,
Thy face, nay more, thy fame is free from soil.
You'll deem this dear, because from me you have it,
I deem your faith more dear, because you gave it.
This pointed diamond cuts glass and steel,
Your love's like force in my firm heart I feel.
But this, as all things else, time wastes with wearing,
Where you my jewels multiply with bearing.

SIR JOHN HARRINGTON

Astrophel and Stella
Sonnet LIV

Because I breathe not love to every one,
    Nor do not use set colours for to wear,
    Nor nourish special locks of vowèd hair,
Nor give each speech a full point of a groan,
The courtly nymphs, acquainted with the moan
Of them which in their lips Love's standard bear,
    'What, he!' say they of me; 'now I dare swear
    He cannot love; no, no, let him alone.'
And think so still, so Stella know my mind!
    Profess, indeed, I do not Cupid's art;
But you, fair maids, at length this true shall find,
    That his right badge is worn but in the heart.
Dumb swans, not chattering pies, do lovers prove;
    They love indeed who quake to say they love.

SIR PHILIP SIDNEY

Bonnie Annie Laurie

Maxwelton's braes are bonnie
Where early fa's the dew
And 'twas there that Annie Laurie
Gave me her promise true
That ne'er forgot shall be
And for Bonnie Annie Laurie
I'd lay me doon and dee.

Her brow is like the snowdrift
Her nape is like the swan
And her face it is the fairest
That ere the sun shone on.
And dark blue is her e'e
And for Bonnie Annie Laurie
I'd lay me doon and dee.

Like dew on the gowan lyin'
Is the fall of her fairy feet
And like winds in the summer sighing
Her voice is low and sweet.

And she's all the world to me
And for Bonnie Annie Laurie
I'd lay me doon and dee.

She's backit like a peacock,
She's breastit like a swan,
She's jimp about the middle,
Her waist ye weill may span;
And she has a rolling eye,
And for bonnie Annie Laurie
I'd lay me doon and dee.

Maxwelton banks are bonnie,
Where early fa's the dew;
Where me and Annie Laurie
Made up the promise true;
And never forget will I,
And for bonny Annie Laurie
I'd lay me doon and dee.

WILLIAM DOUGLAS

Sonnet CXVI

Let me not to the marriage of true minds
Admit impediments. Love is not love
Which alters when it alteration finds,
Or bends with the remover to remove:
O no! it is an ever-fixed mark
That looks on tempests and is never shaken;
It is the star to every wandering bark,
Whose worth's unknown, although his height be taken.
Love's not Time's fool, though rosy lips and cheeks
Within his bending sickle's compass come:
Love alters not with his brief hours and weeks,
But bears it out even to the edge of doom.
If this be error and upon me proved,
I never writ, nor no man ever loved.

WILLIAM SHAKESPEARE

How Do I Love Thee?

From *Sonnets from the Portuguese XLIII*

How do I love thee? Let me count the ways.
I love thee to the depth and breadth and height
My soul can reach, when feeling out of sight
For the ends of Being and ideal Grace.
I love thee to the level of every day's
Most quiet need, by sun and candlelight.
I love thee freely, as men strive for Right;
I love thee purely, as they turn from Praise.
I love with a passion put to use
In my old griefs, and with my childhood's faith.
I love thee with a love I seemed to lose
With my lost saints, – I love thee with the breath,
Smiles, tears, of all my life! and, if God choose,
I shall but love thee better after death.

ELIZABETH BARRETT BROWNING

Break of Day

'Tis true, 'tis day ; what though it be?
O, wilt thou therefore rise from me?
Why should we rise because 'tis light?
Did we lie down because 'twas night?
Love, which in spite of darkness brought us hither,
Should in despite of light keep us together.

Light hath no tongue, but is all eye;
If it could speak as well as spy,
This were the worst that it could say,
That being well I fain would stay,
And that I loved my heart and honour so
That I would not from him, that had them, go.

Must business thee from hence remove?
O! that's the worst disease of love,
The poor, the foul, the false, love can
Admit, but not the busied man.
He which hath business, and makes love, doth do
Such wrong, as when a married man doth woo.

JOHN DONNE

Ah, God, the Way Your Little Finger Moved

Ah, God, the way your little finger moved
As you thrust a bare arm backward
And made play with your hair
And a comb a silly gilt comb
Ah, God – that I should suffer
Because of the way a little finger moved.

STEPHEN CRANE

Chloris in the Snow

I saw fair Chloris walk alone,
When feather'd rain came softly down,
As Jove descending from his Tower
To court her in a silver shower:
The wanton snow flew to her breast,
Like pretty birds into their nest,
But, overcome with whiteness there,
For grief it thaw'd into a tear:
Thence falling on her garments' hem,
To deck her, froze into a gem.

WILLIAM STRODE

To Chloe:
Who For His Sake Wished Herself Younger

There are two births; the one when light
First strikes the new awaken'd sense;
The other when two souls unite,
And we must count our life from thence:
When you loved me and I loved you
Then both of us were born anew.

Love then to us new souls did give
And in those souls did plant new powers;
Since when another life we live,
The breath we breathe is his, not ours:
Love makes those young whom age doth chill,
And whom he finds young keeps young still.

WILLIAM CARTWRIGHT

I Will Make You Brooches

I will make you brooches and toys for your delight
Of bird-song at morning and star-shine at night.
I will make a palace fit for you and me,
Of green days in forests and blue days at sea.

I will make my kitchen, and you shall keep your room,
Where white flows the river and bright blows the broom,
And you shall wash your linen and keep your body white
In rainfall at morning and dewfall at night.

And this shall be for music when no one else is near,
The fine song for singing, the rare song to hear!
That only I remember, that only you admire,
Of the broad road that stretches and the roadside fire.

ROBERT LOUIS STEVENSON

The Indian Serenade

I arise from dreams of thee
In the first sweet sleep of night,
When the winds are breathing low,
And the stars are shining bright.
I arise from dreams of thee,
And a spirit in my feet
Hath led me – who knows how?
To thy chamber window, Sweet!

The wandering airs they faint
On the dark, the silent stream –
And the Champak's odours fail
Like sweet thoughts in a dream;
The nightingale's complaint,
It dies upon her heart,
As I must die on thine,
O belovèd as thou art!

O lift me from the grass!
I die! I faint! I fail!
Let thy love in kisses rain
On my lips and eyelids pale.

My cheek is cold and white, alas!
My heart beats loud and fast:
O press it to thine own again,
Where it will break at last!

PERCY BYSSHE SHELLEY

My True-Love Hath My Heart

My true-love hath my heart and I have his,
By just exchange one for the other given;
I hold his dear and mine he cannot miss;
There never was a better bargain driven.
My true-love hath my heart and I have his.

His heart in me keeps him and me in one;
My heart in him his thoughts and senses guides;
He loves my heart for once it was his own,
I cherish his because in me it bides.
My true-love hath my heart and I have his.

SIR PHILIP SIDNEY

If Thou Must Love Me...

From *Sonnets from the Portuguese XIV*

If thou must love me, let it be for nought
Except for love's sake only. Do not say
'I love her for her smile – her look – her way
Of speaking gently, – for a trick of thought
That falls in well with mine, and certes brought
A sense of pleasant ease on such a day'
For these things in themselves, Beloved, may
Be changed, or change for thee, – and love, so wrought,
May be unwrought so. Neither love me for
Thine own dear pity's wiping my cheeks dry,
A creature might forget to weep, who bore
Thy comfort long, and lose thy love thereby!
But love me for love's sake, that evermore
Thou may'st love on, through love's eternity.

ELIZABETH BARRETT BROWNING

Sonnet XIV

Not from the stars do I my judgement pluck;
And yet methinks I have astronomy,
But not to tell of good or evil luck,
Of plagues, of dearths, or seasons' quality;
Nor can I fortune to brief minutes tell,
Pointing to each his thunder, rain and wind,
Or say with princes if it shall go well,
By oft predict that I in heaven find:
But from thine eyes my knowledge I derive,
And, constant stars, in them I read such art
As truth and beauty shall together thrive,
If from thyself to store thou wouldst convert;
Or else of thee this I prognosticate:
Thy end is truth's and beauty's doom and date.

WILLIAM SHAKESPEARE

Freedom and Love

How delicious is the winning
Of a kiss at love's beginning,
When two mutual hearts are sighing
For the knot there's no untying!
Yet remember, 'midst our wooing,
Love has bliss, but Love has ruing;
Other smiles may make you fickle,
Tears for other charms may trickle.
Love he comes, and Love he tarries,
Just as fate or fancy carries;
Longest stays, when sorest chidden;
Laughs and flies, when press'd and bidden.
Bind the sea to slumber stilly,
Bind its odour to the lily,
Bind the aspen ne'er to quiver,
Then bind Love to last for ever.
Love's a fire that needs renewal
Of fresh beauty for its fuel:
Love's wing moults when caged and captured,
Only free, he soars enraptured.
Can you keep the bee from ranging
Or the ringdove's neck from changing?

No! nor fetter'd Love from dying
In the knot there's no untying.

THOMAS CAMPBELL

The Bracelet: To Julia

Why I tie about thy wrist,
Julia, this silken twist;
For what other reason is
But to show thee how, in part,
Thou my pretty captive art?
But thy bond slave is my heart:
'Tis but silk that bindeth thee,
Knap the thread and thou art free;
But 'tis otherwise with me:
– I am bound and fast bound, so
That from thee I cannot go;
If I could, I would not so.

ROBERT HERRICK

Go and Catch a Falling Star

Go and catch a falling star,
Get with child a mandrake root,
Tell me where all past years are,
Or who cleft the devil's foot,
Teach me to hear mermaids singing,
Or to keep off envy's stinging,
And find
What wind
Serves to advance an honest mind.

If thou be'st born to strange sights,
Things invisible to see,
Ride ten thousand days and nights,
Till age snow white hairs on thee,
Thou, when thou return'st, wilt tell me,
All strange wonders that befell thee,
And swear,
No where
Lives a woman true, and fair.

JOHN DONNE

Marriage

Traditionally, marriage has been the ultimate union towards which lovers aspire – a lifelong commitment to love and nurture 'until death do us part'. This section offers a number of paeans to the love that makes couples want to declare such vows and spend the rest of their lives together.

Marriage Morning

Light, so low upon earth,
You send a flash to the sun.
Here is the golden close of love,
All my wooing is done.
Oh, the woods and the meadows,
Woods where we hid from the wet,
Stiles where we stay'd to be kind,
Meadows in which we met!

Light, so low in the vale
You flash and lighten afar,
For this is the golden morning of love,
And you are his morning star.
Flash, I am coming, I come,
By meadow and stile and wood,
Oh, lighten into my eyes and heart,
Into my heart and my blood!

Heart, are you great enough
For a love that never tires?
O' heart, are you great enough for love?
I have heard of thorns and briers,
Over the meadow and stiles,

Over the world to the end of it
Flash for a million miles.

ALFRED, LORD TENNYSON

Words on Feeling Safe

Oh the comfort of feeling safe
with a person;
having neither to weigh thoughts,
nor measure words,
but to pour them all out
just as chaff and grain together,
knowing that a faithful hand
will take and sift them,
keeping what is worth keeping
and with a breath of kindness,
blow the rest away.

GEORGE ELIOT

The Bridal Veil

We're married, they say, and you think you have won me, –
Well, take this white veil from my head, and look on me;
Here's matter to vex you, and matter to grieve you,
Here's doubt to distrust you, and faith to believe you, –
I am all as you see, common earth, common dew;
Be wary, and mould me to roses, not rue!

Ah! shake out the filmy thing, fold after fold,
And see if you have me to keep and to hold, –
Look close on my heart – see the worst of its sinning, –
It is not yours to-day for the yesterday's winning –
The past is not mine – I am too proud to borrow –
You must grow to new heights if I love you to-morrow.

I have wings flattened down and hid under my veil:
They are subtle as light – you can never undo them,
And swift in their flight – you can never pursue them,
And spite of all clasping, and spite of all bands,
I can slip like a shadow, a dream, from your hands.

Nay, call me not cruel, and fear not to take me,
I am yours for my life-time, to be what you make me, –
To wear my white veil for a sign, or a cover,
As you shall be proven my lord, or my lover;
A cover for peace that is dead, or a token
Of bliss that can never be written or spoken.

ALICE CARY

Wedlock

Wedlock, as old men note, hath likened been,
Unto a public crowd or common rout;
Where those that are without would fain get in,
And those that are within, would fain get out.
Grief often treads upon the heels of pleasure,
Marry'd in haste, we oft repent at leisure;
Some by experience find these words missplaced,
Marry'd at leisure, they repent in haste.

BENJAMIN FRANKLIN

Sonnet III

Look in thy glass, and tell the face thou viewest
Now is the time that face should form another;
Whose fresh repair if now thou not renewest,
Thou dost beguile the world, unbless some mother.
For where is she so fair whose unear'd womb
Disdains the tillage of thy husbandry?
Or who is he so fond will be the tomb
Of his self-love, to stop posterity?
Thou art thy mother's glass, and she in thee
Calls back the lovely April of her prime:
So thou through windows of thine age shall see
Despite of wrinkles this thy golden time.
But if thou live, remember'd not to be,
Die single, and thine image dies with thee.

WILLIAM SHAKESPEARE

To My Dear and Loving Husband

If ever two were one, then surely we.
If ever man were lov'd by wife, then thee.
If ever wife was happy in a man,
Compare with me, ye women, if you can.
I prize thy love more than whole Mines of gold
Or all the riches that the East doth hold.
My love is such that Rivers cannot quench,
Nor aught but love from thee give recompense.
Thy love is such I can no way repay.
The heavens reward thee manifold, I pray.
Then while we live, in love let's so persever
That when we live no more, we may live ever.

ANNE BRADSTREET

The Passionate Shepherd to His Love

Come live with me and be my love,
And we will all the pleasures prove
That valleys, groves, hills, and fields,
Woods, or steepy mountain yields.

And we will sit upon rocks,
Seeing the shepherds feed their flocks,
By shallow rivers to whose falls
Melodious birds sing madrigals.

And I will make thee beds of roses
And a thousand fragrant posies,
A cap of flowers, and a kirtle
Embroidered all with leaves of myrtle;

A gown made of the finest wool
Which from our pretty lambs we pull;
Fair lined slippers for the cold,
With buckles of the purest gold;

A belt of straw and ivy buds,
With coral clasps and amber studs;
And if these pleasures may thee move,
Come live with me, and be my love.

The shepherds's swains shall dance and sing
For thy delight each May morning:
If these delights thy mind may move,
Then live with me and be my love.

CHRISTOPHER MARLOWE

The Nymph's Reply to the Shepherd

If all the world and love were young,
And truth in every shepherd's tongue,
These pretty pleasures might me move
To live with thee and be thy love.

Time drives the flocks from field to fold
When rivers rage and rocks grow cold,
And Philomel becometh dumb;
The rest complains of cares to come.

The flowers do fade, and wanton fields
To wayward winter reckoning yields;
A honey tongue, a heart of gall,
Is fancy's spring, but sorrow's fall.

Thy gowns, thy shoes, thy beds of roses,
Thy cap, thy kirtle, and thy posies
Soon break, soon wither, soon forgotten
In folly ripe, in season rotten.

Thy belt of straw and ivy buds,
Thy coral clasps and amber studs,
All these in me no means can move
To come to thee and be thy love.
But could youth last and love still breed,
Had joys no date nor age no need,
Then these delights my mind might move
To live with thee and be thy love.

SIR WALTER RALEIGH

A Marriage Ring

The ring, so worn as you behold,
So thin, so pale, is yet of gold:
The passion such it was to prove –
Worn with life's care, love yet was love.

GEORGE CRABBE

To a Husband

This is to the crown and blessing of my life,
The much loved husband of a happy wife;
To him whose constant passion found the art
To win a stubborn and ungrateful heart,
And to the world by tenderest proof discovers
They err, who say that husbands can't be lovers.
With such return of passion, as is due,
Daphnis I love, Daphinis my thoughts pursue;
Daphnis, my hopes and joys are bounded all in you.
Even I, for Daphnis' and my promise' sake,
What I in woman censure, undertake.
But this from love, not vanity proceeds;
You know who writes, and I who 'tis that reads.
Judge not my passion by my want of skill:
Many love well, though they express it ill;
And I your censure could with pleasure bear,
Would you but soon return, and speak it here.

ANNE FINCH

Nuptial Sleep

At length their long kiss severed, with sweet smart:
 And as the last slow sudden drops are shed
 From sparkling eaves when all the storm has fled,
 So singly flagged the pulses of each heart.
 Their bosoms sundered, with the opening start
 Of married flowers to either side outspread
From the knit stem; yet still their mouths, burnt red,
 Fawned on each other where they lay apart.

Sleep sank them lower than the tide of dreams,
 And their dreams watched them sink, and slid away.
 Slowly their souls swam up again, through gleams
 Of watered light and dull drowned waifs of day;
 Till from some wonder of new woods and streams
 He woke, and wondered more: for there she lay.

DANTE GABRIEL ROSSETTI

At the Wedding-March

God with honour hang your head,
Groom, and grace you, bride, your bed
With lissome scions, sweet scions,
    Out of hallowed bodies bred.

Each be other's comfort kind:
Déep, déeper than divined,
Divine charity, dear charity,
    Fast you ever, fast bind.

Then let the March tread our ears:
    I to him turn with tears
Who to wedlock, his wonder wedlock,
    Déals tríumph and immortal years.

GERARD MANLEY HOPKINS

The Good-Morrow

I wonder by my troth, what thou and I
Did, till we loved? were we not wean'd till then?

But suck'd on country pleasures, childishly?
Or snorted we in the Seven Sleepers' den?
'Twas so; but this, all pleasures fancies be;
If ever any beauty I did see,
Which I desired, and got, 'twas but a dream of thee.

And now good-morrow to our waking souls,
Which watch not one another out of fear;
For love all love of other sights controls,
And makes one little room an everywhere.
Let sea-discoverers to new worlds have gone;
Let maps to other, worlds on worlds have shown;
Let us possess one world; each hath one, and is one.

My face in thine eye, thine in mine appears,
And true plain hearts do in the faces rest;
Where can we find two better hemispheres
Without sharp north, without declining west?
Whatever dies, was not mix'd equally;
If our two loves be one, or thou and I
Love so alike that none can slacken, none can die.

JOHN DONNE

Before the Birth of One of Her Children

All things within this fading world hath end,
Adversity doth still our joys attend;
No ties so strong, no friends so dear and sweet,
But with death's parting blow is sure to meet.
The sentence past is most irrevocable,
A common thing, yet oh, inevitable.
How soon, my Dear, death may my steps attend.
How soon't may be thy lot to lose thy friend,
We both are ignorant, yet love bids me
These farewell lines to recommend to thee,
That when that knot's untied that made us one,
I may seem thine, who in effect am none.
And if I see not half my days that's due,
What nature would, God grant to yours and you;
The many faults that well you know I have
Let be interred in my oblivious grave;
If any worth or virtue were in me,
Let that live freshly in thy memory
And when thou feel'st no grief, as I no harms,
Yet love thy dead, who long lay in thine arms.
And when thy loss shall be repaid with gains
Look to my little babes, my dear remains.

And if thou love thyself, or loved'st me,
These O protect from step-dame's injury.
And if chance to thine eyes shall bring this verse,
With some sad sighs honour my absent hearse;
And kiss this paper for thy love's dear sake,
Who with salt tears this last farewell did take.

ANNE BRADSTREET

Marriage

The die is cast, come weal, come woe,
Two lives are joined together,
For better or for worse, the link
Which naught but death can sever.
The die is cast, come grief, come joy,
Come richer, or come poorer,
If love but binds the mystic tie,
Blest is the bridal hour.

MARY WESTON FORDHAM

I Gave Myself to Him

I gave myself to him,
And took himself for pay.
The solemn contract of a life
Was ratified this way

The value might disappoint,
Myself a poorer prove
Than this my purchaser suspect,
The daily own of Love

Depreciates the sight;
But, 'til the merchant buy,
Still fabled, in the isles of spice
The subtle cargoes lie.

At least, 'tis mutual risk,
Some found it mutual gain;
Sweet debt of Life, each night to owe,
Insolvent, every noon.

EMILY DICKINSON

Bridal Song

O come, soft rest of cares! come, Night!
   Come, naked Virtue's only tire,
   The reaped harvest of the light
Bound up in sheaves of sacred fire.
     Love calls to war:
     Sighs his alarms,
     Lips his swords are,
     The field his arms.

Come, Night, and lay thy velvet hand
   On glorious Day's outfacing face;
And all thy crowned flames command
   For torches to our nuptial grace.
     Love calls to war:
     Sighs his alarms,
     Lips his swords are,
     The field his arms.

GEORGE CHAPMAN

John Anderson, My Jo

John Anderson, my jo, John,
When we were first acquent;
Your locks were like the raven,
Your bonie brow was brent;
But now your brow is beld, John,
Your locks are like the snaw;
But blessings on your frosty pow,
John Anderson, my jo.

John Anderson, my jo, John,
We clamb the hill thegither;
And mony a cantie day, John,
We've had wi' ane anither:
Now we maun totter down, John,
And hand in hand we'll go,
And sleep thegither at the foot,
John Anderson, my jo.

ROBERT BURNS

To One Persuading a Lady to Marriage

Forbear, bold youth; all's heaven here,
And what you do aver
To others courtship may appear,
'Tis sacrilege to her.
She is a public deity;
And were't not very odd
She should dispose herself to be
A petty household god?

First make the sun in private shine
And bid the world adieu,
That so he may his beams confine
In compliment to you:
But if of that you do despair,
Think how you did amiss
To strive to fix her beams which are
More bright and large than his.

KATHERINE PHILIPS ('ORINDA')

A Letter to Her Husband

My head, my heart, mine eyes, my life, nay more,
My joy, my magazine, of earthly store,
If two be one, as surely thou and I,
How stayest thou there, whilst I at Ipswich lie?
So many steps, head from the heart to sever,
If but a neck, soon should we be together.
I, like the Earth this season, mourn in black,
My Sun is gone so far in's zodiac,
Whom whilst I 'joyed, nor storms, nor frost I felt,
His warmth such fridged colds did cause to melt.
My chilled limbs now numbed lie forlorn;
Return; return, sweet Sol, from Capricorn;
In this dead time, alas, what can I more
Than view those fruits which through thy heart I bore?
Which sweet contentment yield me for a space,
True living pictures of their father's face.
O strange effect! now thou art southward gone,
I weary grow the tedious day so long;
But when thou northward to me shalt return,
I wish my Sun may never set, but burn
Within the Cancer of my glowing breast,
The welcome house of him my dearest guest.

Where ever, ever stay, and go not thence,
Till nature's sad decree shall call thee hence;
Flesh of thy flesh, bone of thy bone,
I here, thou there, yet both but one.

ANNE BRADSTREET

To Silvia, To Wed

Let us, though late, at last, my Silvia, wed;
And loving lie in one devoted bed.
Thy watch may stand, my minutes fly post haste;
No sound calls back the year that once is past.
Then, sweetest Silvia, let's no longer stay;
True love, we know, precipitates delay.
Away with doubts, all scruples hence remove!
No man, at one time, can be wise, and love.

ROBERT HERRICK

Bridal Song

Cynthia, to thy power and thee
We obey.
Joy to this great company!
And no day
Come to steal this night away
Till the rites of love are ended,
And the lusty bridegroom say,
Welcome, light, of all befriended!

Pace out, you watery powers below;
Let your feet,
Like the galleys when they row,
Even beat;
Let your unknown measures, set
To the still winds, tell to all
That gods are come, immortal, great,
To honour this great nuptial!

JOHN FLETCHER

My Wife

Trusty, dusky, vivid, true,
With eyes of gold and bramble-dew,
Steel-true and blade-straight,
The great artificer
Made my mate.

Honour, anger, valour, fire;
A love that life could never tire,
Death quench or evil stir,
The mighty master
Gave to her.

Teacher, tender, comrade, wife,
A fellow-farer true through life,
Heart-whole and soul-free
The august father
Gave to me.

ROBERT LOUIS STEVENSON

To the Virgins, to Make Much of Time

Gather ye rosebuds while ye may,
Old time is still a-flying:
And this same flower that smiles to-day
To-morrow will be dying.

The glorious lamp of heaven, the sun,
The higher he's a-getting,
The sooner will his race be run,
And nearer he's to setting.

That age is best which is the first,
When youth and blood are warmer;
But being spent, the worse, and worst
Times still succeed the former.

Then be not coy, but use your time,
And while ye may go marry:
For having lost but once your prime
You may for ever tarry.

ROBERT HERRICK

Bridal Song

Roses, their sharp spines being gone,
Not royal in their smells alone,
But in their hue;
Maiden pinks, of odour faint,
Daisies smell-less, yet most quaint,
And sweet thyme true;

Primrose, firstborn child of Ver;
Merry springtime's harbinger,
With her bells dim;
Oxlips in their cradles growing,
Marigolds on death-beds blowing,
Larks'-heels trim;

All dear Nature's children sweet
Lie 'fore bride and bridegroom's feet,
Blessing their sense!
Not an angel of the air,
Bird melodious or bird fair,
Be absent hence!

WILLIAM SHAKESPEARE

The Prophet on Marriage

Then Almitra spoke again and said…
'And what of Marriage, master?'
And he answered saying:
You were born together,
and together you shall be forevermore.
You shall be together when the white wings
of death scatter your days.
Aye, you shall be together even in the
silent memory of God.
But let there be spaces in your togetherness,
And let the winds of the heavens dance between you.
Love one another, but make not a bond of love.
Let it rather be a moving sea between
the shores of your souls.
Fill each other's cup but drink not from one cup.
Give one another of your bread but eat not from the same loaf.
Sing and dance together and be joyous,
but let each of you be alone,
Even as the strings of a lute are alone
though they quiver with the same music.
Give your hearts, but not into each other's keeping.

For only the hand of Life can contain your hearts.
And stand together, yet not too near together.
For the pillars of the temple stand apart,
And the oak tree and the cypress
grow not in each other's shadow.

KHALIL GIBRAN

Love is Enough

Love is enough: though the World be a-waning,
And the woods have no voice but the voice of complaining,
Though the sky be too dark for dim eyes to discover
The gold-cups and daisies fair blooming thereunder,
Though the hills be held shadows, and the sea a dark wonder,
And this day draw a veil over all deeds pass'd over,
Yet their hands shall not tremble, their feet shall not falter;
The void shall not weary, the fear shall not alter
These lips and these eyes of the loved and the lover.

WILLIAM MORRIS

The Happy Husband

Oft, oft methinks, the while with Thee
I breath, as from the heart, thy dear
And dedicated name, I hear
A promise and a mystery,
A pledge of more than passing life,
Yea, in that very name of Wife!

A pulse of love, that ne'er can sleep!
A feeling that upbraids the heart
With hapiness beyond desert,
That gladness half requests to weep!
Nor bless I not the keener sense
And unalarming turbulance.

Of transient joys, that ask no sting
From jealous fears, or coy denying;
Bur born beneath Love's brooding wing,
And into tenderness soon dying,
Wheel out their giddy moment, then
Resign the soul to love again; –

A more precipitated vein
Of notes, that eddy in the flow
Of smoothest song, they come, they go,
And leave their sweeter understrain
Its own sweet self – a love of Thee
That seems, yet cannot greater be!

SAMUEL TAYLOR COLERIDGE

Traditional Gaelic Blessing

May the road rise up to meet you.
May the wind be always at your back.
May the sun shine warm upon your face;
the rains fall soft upon your fields and until we meet again,
may God hold you in the palm of His hand.

ANONYMOUS

Satires of Circumstance
I. At Tea

The kettle descants in a cosy drone,
And the young wife looks in her husband's face,
And then at her guest's, and shows in her own
Her sense that she fills an envied place;
And the visiting lady is all abloom,
And says there was never so sweet a room.

And the happy young housewife does not know
That the woman beside her was first his choice,
Till the fates ordained it could not be so…
Betraying nothing in look or voice
The guest sits smiling and sips her tea,
And he throws her a stray glance yearningly.

THOMAS HARDY

Sonnet VIII

Music to hear, why hear'st thou music sadly?
Sweets with sweets war not, joy delights in joy.
Why lovest thou that which thou receivest not gladly,
Or else receivest with pleasure thine annoy?
If the true concord of well-tuned sounds,
By unions married, do offend thine ear,
They do but sweetly chide thee, who confounds
In singleness the parts that thou shouldst bear.
Mark how one string, sweet husband to another,
Strikes each in each by mutual ordering,
Resembling sire and child and happy mother
Who all in one, one pleasing note do sing:
Whose speechless song, being many, seeming one,
Sings this to thee: 'thou single wilt prove none.'

WILLIAM SHAKESPEARE

The Wedding Night

Within the chamber, far away

From the glad feast, sits Love in dread
Lest guests disturb, in wanton play,

The silence of the bridal bed.
His torch's pale flame serves to gild

The scene with mystic sacred glow;
The room with incense-clouds is fil'd,

That ye may perfect rapture know.

How beats thy heart, when thou dost hear

The chime that warns thy guests to fly!
How glow'st thou for those lips so dear,

That soon are mute, and nought deny!
With her into the holy place

Thou hast'nest then, to perfect all;
The fire the warder's hands embrace,

Grows, like a night-light, dim and small.

How heaves her bosom, and how burns

Her face at every fervent kiss!
Her coldness now to trembling turns,

Thy daring now a duty is.
Love helps thee to undress her fast,

But thou art twice as fast as he;
And then he shuts both eye at last,

With sly and roguish modesty.

JOHANN WOLFGANG VON GOETHE

Ruth

She stood breast-high amid the corn,
Clasp'd by the golden light of morn,
    Like the sweetheart of the sun,
Who many a glowing kiss had won.

    On her cheek an autumn flush,
    Deeply ripen'd; – such a blush
    In the midst of brown was born,
Like red poppies grown with corn.

    Round her eyes her tresses fell,
Which were blackest none could tell,
    But long lashes veil'd a light,
That had else been all too bright.

    And her hat, with shady brim,
    Made her tressy forehead dim;
    Thus she stood amid the stooks,
Praising God with sweetest looks: –

Sure, I said, Heav'n did not mean,
Where I reap thou shouldst but glean,
Lay thy sheaf adown and come,
Share my harvest and my home.

THOMAS HOOD

The Angel in the House
An Excerpt

Across the sky the daylight crept,
And birds grew garrulous in the grove,
And on my marriage-morn I slept
A soft sleep, undisturb'd by love.

COVENTRY PATMORE

Satires of Circumstance
IX. At the Altar-Rail

'My bride is not coming, alas!' says the groom,
  And the telegram shakes in his hand. 'I own
It was hurried! We met at a dancing-room
  When I went to the Cattle-Show alone,
And then, next night, where the Fountain leaps,
And the Street of the Quarter-Circle sweeps.

'Ay, she won me to ask her to be my wife –
  'Twas foolish perhaps! – to forsake the ways
Of the flaring town for a farmer's life.
  She agreed. And we fixed it. Now she says:
"It's sweet of you, dear, to prepare me a nest,
  But a swift, short, gay life suits me best.
What I really am you have never gleaned;
I had eaten the apple ere you were weaned."'

THOMAS HARDY

Unrequited Love

The sweet pain of loving another, but not being loved
in return, is one of life's great paradoxes. There is, of
course, always hope, but as Andrew Marvell writes in
The Definition of Love, sometimes the poet – and the
reader – has to become resigned to the fact that love
can be futile. As Marvell writes, his love will never
happen 'Unless the giddy heaven fall
And earth some new convulsion tear'.

I Loved You Once

I loved you once, nor can this heart be quiet;
For it would seem that love still lingers there;
But do not you be further troubled by it;
I would in no wise hurt you, oh, my dear.

I loved you without hope, a mute offender;
What jealous pangs, what shy despairs I knew!
A love as deep as this, as true, as tender,
God grant another may yet offer you.

ALEXANDER PUSHKIN

Proud of My Broken Heart

Proud of my broken heart since thou didst break it,
Proud of the pain I did not feel till thee,
Proud of my night since thou with moons dost slake it,
Not to partake thy passion, my humility.

EMILY DICKINSON

If Grief For Grief Can Touch Thee

If grief for grief can touch thee,
If answering woe for woe,
If any truth can melt thee
Come to me now!

I cannot be more lonely,
More drear I cannot be!
My worn heart beats so wildly
'Twill break for thee –

And when the world despises –
When Heaven repels my prayer –
Will not mine angel comfort?
Mine idol hear?

Yes, by the tears I'm poured,
By all my hours of pain
O I shall surely win thee,
Beloved, again!

EMILY BRONTË

Go, Lovely Rose

Go, lovely rose –
Tell her that wastes her time, and me,
That now she knows,
When I resemble her to thee,
How sweet and fair she seems to be.

Tell her that's young,
And shuns to have her graces spied,
That hadst thou sprung
In deserts where no men abide,
Thou must have uncommended died.

Small is the worth
Of beauty from the light retired:
Bid her come forth,
Suffer herself to be desired,
And not blush so to be admired.

Then die – that she
The common fate of all things rare
May read in thee
How small a part of time they share
That are so wondrous sweet, and fair!

EDMUND WALLER

Why the Roses are so Pale

Oh Dearest, canst thou tell me why
    The rose should be so pale?
    And why the azure violet
    Should wither in the vale?

And why the lark should in the cloud
    So sorrowfully sing?
And why from loveliest balsam-buds
    A scent of death should spring?

And why the sun upon the mead
    So chillingly should frown?
And why the earth should, like a grave,
    Be moldering and brown?

And why it is that I myself
    So languishing should be?
And why it is, my heart of hearts,
    That thou forsakest me?

HEINRICH HEINE

Vivien's Song

'In Love, if Love be Love, if Love be ours,
Faith and unfaith can ne'er be equal powers:
Unfaith in aught is want of faith in all.

It is the little rift within the lute,
That by and by will make the music mute,
And ever widening slowly silence all.

The little rift within the lover's lute,
Or little pitted speck in garner'd fruit,
That rotting inward slowly moulders all.

It is not worth the keeping: let it go;
But shall it? answer, darling, answer, no.
And trust me not at all or all in all.'

ALFRED, LORD TENNYSON

Love Arm'd

Love in fantastic triumph sat,
Whilst bleeding hearts around him flow'd,
For whom fresh pains he did create,
And strange tyrannic power he show'd;
From thy bright eyes he took his fire,
Which round about, in sport he hurl'd;
But 'twas from mine he took desire,
Enough to undo the amorous world.
From me he took his sighs and tears,
From thee his pride and cruelty;
From me his languishments and fears,
And every killing dart from thee;
Thus thou and I, the god have arm'd,
And set him up a deity;
But my poor heart alone is harm'd,
Whilst thine the victor is, and free.

APHRA BEHN

Renouncement

I must not think of thee; and, tired yet strong,
    I shun the love that lurks in all delight –
The love of thee – and in the blue heaven's height,
        And in the dearest passage of a song.
Oh, just beyond the sweetest thoughts that throng
This breast, the thought of thee waits hidden yet bright;
        But it must never, never come in sight;
    I must stop short of thee the whole day long.
But when sleep comes to close each difficult day,
    When night gives pause to the long watch I keep,
    And all my bonds I needs must loose apart,
        Must doff my will as raiment laid away, –
With the first dream that comes with the first sleep
    I run, I run, I am gather'd to thy heart.

ALICE MEYNELL

My Heart was Slain

My heart was slain, and none but you and I;
Who should I think the murther should commit,
Since but yourself there was no creature by,
But only I, guiltless of murth'ring it?
It slew itself; the verdict on the view
Doth quit the dead, and me not accessary.
Well, well, I fear it will be prov'd by you,
The evidence so great a proof doth carry.
But O, see, see, we need inquire no further:
Upon your lips the scarlet drops are found,
And in your eye the boy that did the murther;
Your cheeks yet pale, since first he gave the wound.
By this I see, however things be past,
Yet Heaven will still have murther out at last.

MICHAEL DRAYTON

The Definition of Love

My love is of a birth as rare
As 'tis for object strange and high;
It was begotten by Despair
Upon Impossibility.

Magnanimous Despair alone
Could show me so divine a thing
Where feeble Hope could ne'er have flown,
But vainly flapp'd its tinsel wing.

And yet I quickly might arrive
Where my extended soul is fixt,
But Fate does iron wedges drive,
And always crowds itself betwixt.

For Fate with jealous eye does see
Two perfect loves, nor lets them close;
Their union would her ruin be,
And her tyrannic pow'r depose.

And therefore her decrees of steel
Us as the distant poles have plac'd,
(Though love's whole world on us doth wheel)
Not by themselves to be embrac'd;

Unless the giddy heaven fall,
And earth some new convulsion tear;
And, us to join, the world should all
Be cramp'd into a planisphere.

As lines, so loves oblique may well
Themselves in every angle greet;
But ours so truly parallel,
Though infinite, can never meet.

Therefore the love which us doth bind,
But Fate so enviously debars,
Is the conjunction of the mind,
And opposition of the stars.

ANDREW MARVELL

Song to Celia

Drink to me, only with thine eyes
And I will pledge with mine;
Or leave a kiss but in the cup,
And I'll not look for wine.
The thirst that from the soul doth rise
Doth ask a drink divine:
But might I of Jove's nectar sup
I would not change for thine.

I sent thee late a rosy wreath,
Not so much honouring thee
As giving it a hope that there
It could not withered be
But thou thereon didst only breath
And sent'st it back to me:
Since, when it grows and smells, I swear,
Not of itself but thee.

BEN JONSON

Like the Touch of Rain

Like the touch of rain she was
On a man's flesh and hair and eyes
When the joy of walking thus
Has taken him by surprise:

With the love of the storm he burns,
He sings, he laughs, well I know how,
But forgets when he returns
As I shall not forget her 'Go now'.

Those two words shut a door
Between me and the blessed rain
That was never shut before
And will not open again.

EDWARD THOMAS

A Dream Within a Dream

Take this kiss upon the brow!
And, in parting from you now,
Thus much let me avow –
You are not wrong, who deem
That my days have been a dream;
Yet if hope has flown away
In a night, or in a day,
In a vision, or in none,
Is it therefore the less gone?
All that we see or seem
Is but a dream within a dream.

I stand amid the roar
Of a surf-tormented shore,
And I hold within my hand
Grains of the golden sand –
How few! yet how they creep
Through my fingers to the deep,
While I weep – while I weep!
O God! can I not grasp
Them with a tighter clasp?
O God! can I not save
One from the pitiless wave?

Is all that we see or seem
But a dream within a dream?

EDGAR ALLAN POE

Amoretti
Sonnet XXX

My love is like to ice, and I to fire;
How comes it then that this her cold so great
Is not dissolved through my so-hot desire,
But harder grows the more I her entreat?
Or how comes it that my exceeding heat
Is not allayed by her heart-frozen cold,
But that I burn much more in boiling sweat,
And feel my flames augmented manifold?
What more miraculous thing may be told,
That fire, which all things melts, should harden ice,
And ice, which is congeal's with senseless cold,
Should kindle fire by wonderful device?
Such is the power of love in gentle mind,
That it can alter all the course of kind.

EDMUND SPENSER

Coldness in Love

And you remember, in the afternoon
The sea and the sky went grey, as if there had sunk
A flocculent dust on the floor of the world: the festoon
Of the sky sagged dusty as spider cloth,
And coldness clogged the sea, till it ceased to croon.

A dank, sickening scent came up from the grime
Of weed that blackened the shore, so that I recoiled
Feeling the raw cold dun me: and all the time
You leapt about on the slippery rocks, and threw
The words that rang with a brassy, shallow chime.

And all day long that raw and ancient cold
Deadened me through, till the grey downs darkened to sleep.
Then I longed for you with your mantle of love to fold
Me over, and drive from out of my body the deep
Cold that had sunk to my soul, and there kept hold.

But still to me all evening long you were cold,
And I was numb with a bitter, deathly ache;
Till old days drew me back into their fold,

And dim sheep crowded me warm with companionship,
And old ghosts clustered me close, and sleep was cajoled.

I slept till dawn at the window blew in like dust,
Like the linty, raw-cold dust disturbed from the floor
Of a disused room: a grey pale light like must
That settled upon my face and hands till it seemed
To flourish there, as pale mould blooms on a crust.

Then I rose in fear, needing you fearfully,
For I thought you were warm as a sudden jet of blood.
I thought I could plunge in your spurting hotness, and be
Clean of the cold and the must. With my hand on the latch
I heard you in your sleep speak strangely to me.

And I dared not enter, feeling suddenly dismayed.
So I went and washed my deadened flesh in the sea
And came back tingling clean, but worn and frayed
With cold, like the shell of the moon: and strange it seems
That my love has dawned in rose again, like the love of a maid.

D. H. LAWRENCE

The December Rose

Here's a rose that blows for Chloe,
Fair as ever a rose in June was,
Now the garden's silent, snowy,
Where the burning summer noon was.

In your garden's summer glory
One poor corner, shelved and shady,
Told no rosy, radiant story,
Grew no rose to grace its lady.

What shuts sun out shuts out snow too;
From his nook your secret lover
Shows what slighted roses grow to
When the rose you chose is over.

EDITH NESBIT

The Silent Lover

Wrong not, sweet empress of my heart,
The merit of true passion,
With thinking that he feels no smart,
That sues for no compassion.

Silence in love bewrays more woe
Than words, though ne'er so witty:
A beggar that is dumb, you know,
May challenge double pity.

Then wrong not, dearest to my heart,
My true, though secret passion;
He smarteth most that hides his smart,
And sues for no compassion.

SIR WALTER RALEIGH

Song

She is not fair to outward view
As many maidens be,
Her loveliness I never knew
Until she smiled on me;
O, then I saw her eye was bright,
A well of love, a spring of light!

But now her looks are coy and cold,
To mine they ne'er reply,
And yet I cease not to behold
The love-light in her eye;
Her very frowns are fairer far
Than smiles of other maidens are.

HARTLEY COLERIDGE

Love's Secret

Never seek to tell thy love,
Love that never told can be;
For the gentle wind does move
Silently, invisibly.

I told my love, I told my love,
I told her all my heart;
Trembling, cold, in ghastly fears,
Ah! she did depart!

Soon as she was gone from me,
A traveller came by,
Silently, invisibly
He took her with a sigh.

WILLIAM BLAKE

Damelus' Song to Diaphenia

Diaphenia, like the daffadowndilly,
White as the sun, fair as the lily,
Heigh ho, how I do love thee!
I do love thee as my lambs
Are belovëd of their dams –
How blest were I if thou wouldst prove me!

Diaphenia, like the spreading roses,
That in thy sweets all sweets incloses,
Fair sweet, how I do love thee!
I do love thee as each flower
Loves the sun's life-giving power,
For, dead, thy breath to life might move me.

Diaphenia, like to all things blessed,
When all thy praises are expressëd,
Dear joy, how I do love thee!
As the birds do love the spring,
Or the bees their careful king, –
Then in requite, sweet virgin, love me!

HENRY CONSTABLE

One Way of Love

All June I bound the rose in sheaves.
Now, rose by rose, I strip the leaves
And strew them where Pauline may pass.
She will not turn aside? Alas!
Let them lie. Suppose they die?
The chance was they might take her eye.

How many a month I strove to suit
These stubborn fingers to the lute!
To-day I venture all I know.
She will not hear my music? So!
Break the string; fold music's wing:
Suppose Pauline had bade me sing!

My whole life long I learned to love.
This hour my utmost art I prove
And speak my passion – heaven or hell?
She will not give me heaven? 'Tis well!
Lose who may – I still can say,
Those who win heaven, blest are they!

ROBERT BROWNING

Tell Me No More

Tell me no more how fair she is,
I have no minde to hear
The story of that distant bliss
I never shall come near:
By sad experience I have found
That her perfection is my wound.
And tell me not how fond I am
To tempt a daring Fate,
From whence no triumph ever came,
But to repent too late:
There is some hope ere long I may
In silence dote my self away.
I ask no pity (Love) from thee,
Nor will thy justice blame,
So that thou wilt not envy mee
The glory of my flame:
Which crowns my heart when ere it dyes,
In that it falls her sacrifice.

HENRY KING

Love's Philosophy

The fountains mingle with the river,
And the rivers with the ocean;
The winds of heaven mix forever,
With a sweet emotion;
Nothing in the world is single;
All things by a law divine
In one another's being mingle; –
Why not I with thine?

See, the mountains kiss high heaven,
And the waves clasp one another;
No sister flower would be forgiven,
If it disdained it's brother;
And the sunlight clasps the earth,
And the moonbeams kiss the sea; –
What are all these kissings worth,
If thou kiss not me?

PERCY BYSSHE SHELLEY

To Mary

I sleep with thee, and wake with thee,
And yet thou art not there;
I fill my arms with thoughts of thee,
And press the common air.
Thy eyes are gazing upon mine,
When thou art out of sight;
My lips are always touching thine,
At morning, noon, and night.

I think and speak of other things
To keep my mind at rest:
But still to thee my memory clings
Like love in woman's breast.
I hide it from the world's wide eye,
And think and speak contrary;
But soft the wind comes from the sky,
And whispers tales of Mary.

The night wind whispers in my ear,
The moons shines in my face;
A burden still of chilling fear
I find in every place.

The breeze is whispering in the bush,
And the dews fall from the tree,
All sighing on, and will not hush,
Some pleasant tales of thee.

JOHN CLARE

To Electra

I dare not ask a kiss,
I dare not beg a smile,
Lest having that, or this,
I might grow proud the while.

No, no, the utmost share
Of my desire shall be
Only to kiss that air
That lately kissed thee.

ROBERT HERRICK

I Prithee Send Me Back My Heart

I prithee send me back my heart,
Since I cannot have thine;
For if from yours you will not part,
Why, then, shouldst thou have mine?

Yet now I think on't, let it lie,
To find it were in vain;
For thou hast a thief in either eye
Would steal it back again.

Why should two hearts in one breast lie,
And yet not lodge together?
O Love! where is thy sympathy,
If thus our breasts thou sever?

But love is such a mystery,
I cannot find it out;
For when I think I'm best resolved,
I then am in most doubt.

Then farewell care, and farewell woe;
I will no longer pine;
For I'll believe I have her heart,
As much as she hath mine.

SIR JOHN SUCKLING

To a Stranger

Passing stranger! you do not know
How longingly I look upon you,
You must be he I was seeking,
Or she I was seeking
(It comes to me as a dream)

I have somewhere surely
Lived a life of joy with you,
All is recall'd as we flit by each other,
Fluid, affectionate, chaste, matured,

You grew up with me,
Were a boy with me or a girl with me,
I ate with you and slept with you, your body has become
not yours only nor left my body mine only,

You give me the pleasure of your eyes, face, flesh as we pass,
You take of my beard, breast, hands, in return,

I am not to speak to you, I am to think of you
when I sit alone or wake at night, alone
I am to wait, I do not doubt I am to meet you again
I am to see to it that I do not lose you.

WALT WHITMAN

Song

You say you love; but with a voice
Chaster than a nun's, who singeth
The soft vespers to herself
While the chime-bell ringeth –
O love me truly!

You say you love; but with a smile
Cold as sunrise in September,
As you were Saint Cupid's nun,
And kept his weeks of Ember –
O love me truly!

You say you love; but then your lips
Coral tinted teach no blisses,
More than coral in the sea –
They never pout for kisses –
O love me truly!

You say you love; but then your hand
No soft squeeze for squeeze returneth;
It is, like a statue's, dead, –
While mine to passion burneth –
O love me truly!

O breathe a word or two of fire!
Smile, as if those words should burn me,
Squeeze as lovers should – O kiss
And in thy heart inurn me –
O love me truly!

JOHN KEATS

To the Western Wind

Sweet western wind, whose luck it is,
Made rival with the air,
To give Perenna's lip a kiss,
And fan her wanton hair.

Bring me but one, I'll promise thee,
Instead of common showers.
Thy wings shall be enbalm'd by me,
And all beset with flowers.

ROBERT HERRICK

To His Coy Love

I pray thee, leave, love me no more,
Call home the heart you gave me!
I but in vain that saint adore
That can but will not save me.
These poor half-kisses kill me quite –
Was ever man thus served?
Amidst an ocean of delight
For pleasure to be starved?

Show me no more those snowy breasts
With azure riverets branched,
Where, whilst mine eye with plenty feasts,
Yet is my thirst not stanched;
O Tantalus, thy pains ne'er tell!
By me thou art prevented:
'Tis nothing to be plagued in Hell,
But thus in Heaven tormented.

Clip me no more in those dear arms,
Nor thy life's comfort call me,
O these are but too powerful charms,
And do but more enthral me!

But see how patient I am grown
In all this coil about thee:
Come, nice thing, let my heart alone,
I cannot live without thee!

MICHAEL DRAYTON

Proud Word You Never Spoke

Proud word you never spoke, but you will speak
Four not exempt from pride some future day.
Resting on one white hand a warm wet cheek,
Over my open volume you will say,
'This man loved me' – then rise and trip away.

WALTER SAVAGE LANDOR

Encouragements to a Lover

Why so pale and wan, fond lover?
　　Prythee, why so pale?
Will, if looking well can't move her,
　　Looking ill prevail?
　　Prythee, why so pale?

Why so dull and mute, young sinner?
　　Prythee, why so mute?
Will, when speaking well can't win her,
　　Saying nothing do't?
　　Prythee, why so mute?

Quit, quit, for shame! this will not move,
　　This cannot take her;
If of herself she will not love,
　　Nothing can make her:
　　The Devil take her!

SIR JOHN SUCKLING

Astrophel and Stella
Sonnet XIX

On Cupid's bow how are my heartstrings bent,
That see my wrack, and yet embrace the same?
When most I glory, then I feel most shame:
I willing run, yet while I run, repent.
My best wits still their own disgrace invent:
My very ink turns straight to Stella's name;
And yet my words, as them my pen doth frame,
Avise themselves that they are vainly spent.
For though she pass all things, yet what is all
That unto me, who fare like him that both
Looks to the skies and in a ditch doth fall?
Oh let me prop my mind, yet in his growth,
And not in Nature, for best fruits unfit:
'Scholar,' saith Love, 'bend hitherward your wit.'

SIR PHILIP SIDNEY

There is a Lady Sweet and Kind

There is a lady sweet and kind,
Was never face so pleas'd my mind;
I did but see her passing by,
And yet I love her till I die.

Her gesture, motion, and her smiles,
Her wit, her voice, my heart beguiles,
Beguiles my heart, I know not why,
And yet I love her till I die.

Her free behaviour, winning looks,
Will make a lawyer burn his books;
I touch'd her not, alas! not I,
And yet I love her till I die.

Had I her fast betwixt mine arms,
Judge you that think such sports were harms,
Were't any harm? no, no, fie, fie,
For I will love her till I die.

Should I remain confined there
So long as Phœbus in his sphere,
I to request, she to deny,
Yet would I love her till I die.

Cupid is winged and doth range,
Her country so my love doth change:
But change she earth, or change she sky,
Yet will I love her till I die.

THOMAS FORD

Astrophel and Stella
Sonnet XXXI

With how sad steps, O moon, thou climb'st the skies!
How silently, and with how wan a face!
What! may it be that even in heavenly place
That busy archer his sharp arrows tries?
Sure, if that long-with-love-acquainted eyes
Can judge of love, thou feel'st a lover's case:
I read it in thy looks; thy languish'd grace
To me, that feel the like, thy state descries.
Then, even of fellowship, O Moon, tell me,
Is constant love deem'd there but want of wit?
Are beauties there as proud as here they be?
Do they above love to be loved, and yet
Those lovers scorn whom that love doth possess?
Do they call 'virtue' there – ungratefulness?

SIR PHILIP SIDNEY

She Dwelt Among Untrodden Ways

She dwelt among the untrodden ways
Beside the springs of Dove,
Maid whom there were none to praise
And very few to love:

A violet by a mosy tone
Half hidden from the eye!
– Fair as a star, when only one
Is shining in the sky.

She lived unknown, and few could know
When Lucy ceased to be;
But she is in her grave, and, oh,
The difference to me!

WILLIAM WORDSWORTH

A Broken Appointment

You did not come,
And marching Time drew on, and wore me numb.
Yet less for loss of your dear presence there
Than that I thus found lacking in your make
That high compassion which can overbear
Reluctance for pure loving kindness' sake
Grieved I, when, as the hope-hour stroked its sum,
You did not come.

You love not me,
And love alone can lend you loyalty;
– I know and knew it. But, unto the store
Of human deeds divine in all but name,
Was it not worth a little hour or more
To add yet this: Once you, a woman, came
To soothe a time-torn man; even though it be
You love not me.

THOMAS HARDY

Life in a Love

Escape me?
Never
Beloved!
While I am I, and you are you,
So long as the world contains us both,
Me the loving and you the loth,
While the one eludes, must the other pursue.
My life is a fault at last, I fear:
It seems too much like a fate, indeed!
Though I do my best I shall scarce succeed.
But what if I fail of my purpose here?
It is but to keep the nerves at strain,
To dry one's eyes and laugh at a fall,
And baffled, get up to begin again,
So the chase takes up one's life, that's all.
While, look but once from your farthest bound,
At me so deep in the dust and dark,
No sooner the old hope drops to ground
Than a new one, straight to the selfsame mark,
I shape me
Ever
Removed!

ROBERT BROWNING

Love Lies Bleeding

You call it, 'Love lies bleeding,' – so you may,
Though the red Flower, not prostrate, only droops,
As we have seen it here from day to day,
From month to month, life passing not away:
A flower how rich in sadness! Even thus stoops,
(Sentient by Grecian sculpture's marvellous power)
Thus leans, with hanging brow and body bent
Earthward in uncomplaining languishment
The dying Gladiator. So, sad Flower!
('Tis Fancy guides me willing to be led,
Though by a slender thread,)
So drooped Adonis bathed in sanguine dew
Of his death-wound, when he from innocent air
The gentlest breath of resignation drew;
While Venus in a passion of despair
Rent, weeping over him, her golden hair
Spangled with drops of that celestial shower.
She suffered, as Immortals sometimes do;
But pangs more lasting far, that Lover knew
Who first, weighed down by scorn, in some lone bower
Did press this semblance of unpitied smart
Into the service of his constant heart,
His own dejection, downcast Flower! could share
With thine, and gave the mournful name
which thou wilt ever bear.

WILLIAM WORDSWORTH

Long-distance Love

The pain of separation from a loved one can be one of the most intense feelings we experience. Even being apart for a night can be as painful as being parted for years. This section contains consummate poems of lovelorn separation such as Byron's *When We Two Parted* and Hart Crane's *Carrier Letter*, verses to ease the pain of distant love.

I Am Shut Out of Mine Own Heart

I am shut out of mine own heart
because my love is far from me,
nor in the wonders have I part
that fill its hidden empery:

The wildwood of adventurous thought
and lands of dawn my dream had won,
the riches out of Faery brought
are buried with our bridal sun.

And I am in a narrow place,
and all its little streets are cold,
because the absence of her face
has robb'd the sullen air of gold.

My home is in a broader day:
at times I catch it glistening
thro' the dull gate, a flower'd play
and odour of undying spring:

The long days that I lived alone,
sweet madness of the springs I miss'd,

are shed beyond, and thro' them blown
clear laughter, and my lips are kiss'd:

– and here, from mine own joy apart,
I wait the turning of the key: –
I am shut out of mine own heart
because my love is far from me.

CHRISTOPHER BRENNAN

Silent is the House

Come, the wind may never again
Blow as now it blows for us;
And the stars may never again shine as now they shine;
Long before October returns,
Seas of blood will have parted us;
And you must crush the love in your heart,
and I the love in mine!

EMILY BRONTË

A Farewell

With all my will, but much against my heart,
We two now part.
My Very Dear,
Our solace is, the sad road lies so clear.
It needs no art,
With faint, averted feet
And many a tear,
In our opposed paths to persevere.
Go thou to East, I West.
We will not say
There's any hope, it is so far away.
But, O, my Best,
When the one darling of our widowhead,
The nursling Grief,
Is dead,
And no dews blur our eyes
To see the peach-bloom come in evening skies,
Perchance we may,
Where now this night is day,
And even through faith of still averted feet,
Making full circle of our banishment,
Amazed meet;
The bitter journey to the bourne so sweet

Seasoning the termless feast of our content
With tears of recognition never dry.

COVENTRY PATMORE

Amoretti
Sonnet LXXXIX

Like as the culver, on the barèd bough,
Sits mourning for the absence of her mate;
And, in her songs, sends many a wishful vow
For his return that seems to linger late:
So I alone, now left disconsolate,
Mourn to myself the absence of my love;
And, wandering here and there all desolate,
Seek with my plaints to match that mournful dove
Ne joy of aught that under heaven doth hove,
Can comfort me, but her own joyous sight
Whose sweet aspect both God and man can move,
In her unspotted pleasance to delight.
Dark is my day, whiles her fair light I miss,
And dead my life that wants such lively bliss.

EDMUND SPENSER

Complaint of the Absence of Her Love Being Upon the Sea

O happy dames, that may embrace
The fruit of your delight,
Help to bewail the woeful case
And eke the heavy plight
Of me, that wonted to rejoice
The fortune of my pleasant choice;
Good ladies, help to fill my mourning voice.

In ship, freight with remembrance
Of thoughts and pleasures past,
He sails that hath in governance
My life while it will last;
With scalding sighs, for lack of gale,
Furthering his hope, that is his sail,
Toward me, the sweet port of his avail.

Alas! how oft in dreams I see
Those eyes that were my food;
Which sometime so delighted me,
That yet they do me good;
Wherewith I wake with his return,
Whose absent flame did make me burn:
But when I find the lack, Lord, how I mourn!

When other lovers in arms across
Rejoice their chief delight.
Drowned in tears, to mourn my loss
I stand the bitter night
In my window, where I may see
Before the winds how the clouds flee.
Lo! what a mariner love hath made of me!

And in green waves when the salt flood
Doth rise by rage of wind,
A thousand fancies in that mood
Assail my restless mind.
Alas! now drencheth my sweet foe,
That with the spoil of my heart did go,
And left me; but, alas! why did he so?

And when the seas wax calm again
To chase fro me annoy,
My doubtful hope doth cause me pain;
So dread cuts off my joy.
Thus is my wealth mingled with woe,
And of each thought a doubt doth grow;
'Now he comes! Will he come? Alas, no, no!'

HENRY HOWARD, EARL OF SURREY

I Leave Thee for Awhile

I leave thee for awhile, my love, I leave thee with a sigh;
The fountain spring within my soul is playing in mine eye;
I do not blush to own the tear, – let, let it touch my cheek,
And what my lip has failed to tell, that drop perchance
may speak.
Mavourneen! when again I seek my green isle in the West,
Oh, promise thou wilt share my lot, and set this heart at rest.

I leave thee for awhile, my love; but every hour will be
Uncheered and lonely till the one that brings me back to thee.
I go to make my riches more; but where is man to find
A vein of gold so rich and pure as that I leave behind?
Mavourneen! though my home might be the fairest
earth possessed,
Till thou wouldst share and make it warm, this heart would
know no rest.

I leave thee for awhile, my love; my cheek is cold and white,
But ah, I see a promise stand within thy glance of light;
When next I seek old, Erin's shore, thy step will bless it too,
And then the grass will seem more green, the sky will
have more blue.

Mavourneen! first and dearest loved, there's sunshine
in my breast,
For thou wilt share my future lot, and set this heart at rest.

ELIZA COOK

Carrier Letter

My hands have not touched water since your hands, –
No; – nor my lips freed laughter since 'farewell'.
And with the day, distance again expands
Between us, voiceless as an uncoiled shell.

Yet, – much follows, much endures… Trust birds alone:
A dove's wings clung about my heart last night
With surging gentleness; and the blue-stone
Set in the tryst-ring has but worn more bright.

HART CRANE

When We Two Parted

When we two parted
In silence and tears,
Half broken-hearted
To sever for years,
Pale grew thy cheek and cold,
Colder thy kiss;
Truly that hour foretold
Sorrow to this.

The dew of the morning
Sunk chill on my brow –
It felt like the warning
Of what I feel now.
Thy vows are all broken,
And light is thy fame;
I hear thy name spoken,
And share in its shame.

They name thee before me,
A knell to mine ear;
A shrudder comes o'er me –
Why wert thou so dear?
They know not I knew thee,
Who knew thee so well –
Long, long I shall rue thee,
Too deeply to tell.

In secret we met –
In silence I grieve,
That thy heart could forget,
Thy spirit deceive
If I should meet thee
After long years,
How should I greet thee? –
With silence and tears.

GEORGE GORDON, LORD BYRON

Song to a Fair Young Lady, Going Out of the Town in the Spring

Ask not the cause why sullen Spring
So long delays her flowers to bear;
Why warbling birds forget to sing,
And winter storms invert the year:
Chloris is gone; and fate provides
To make it Spring where she resides.

Chloris is gone, the cruel fair;
She cast not back a pitying eye:
But left her lover in despair
To sigh, to languish, and to die:
Ah! how can those fair eyes endure
To give the wounds they will not cure?

Great God of Love, why hast thou made
A face that can all hearts command,
That all religions can invade,
And change the laws of every land?
Where thou hadst plac'd such power before,
Thou shouldst have made her mercy more.

When Chloris to the temple comes,
Adoring crowds before her fall;
She can restore the dead from tombs
And every life but mine recall.
I only am by Love design'd
To be the victim for mankind.

JOHN DRYDEN

Echoes and Memories

Music, when soft voices die,
Vibrates in the memory –
Odors, when sweet violets sicken,
Live within the sense they quicken.

Rose leaves, when the rose is dead,
Are heaped for the beloved's bed;
And so thy thoughts, when thou art gone,
Love itself shall slumber on.

PERCY BYSSHE SHELLEY

To Althea, From Prison

When Love with unconfinèd wings
    Hovers within my gates;
And my divine Althea brings
    To whisper at the grates;
When I lye tangled in her haire
    And fettered to her eye;
The gods that wanton in the air,
    Know no such liberty.

When flowing cups run swiftly round
    With no allaying Thames,
Our careless heads with roses bound,
    Our hearts with loyal flames;
When thirsty grief in wine we steep,
When healths and draughts go free,
    Fishes that tipple in the deep,
    Know no such liberty.

When, like committed linnets, I
With shriller throat shall sing
The sweetnes, mercy, majesty,
And glories of my King;
When I shall voice aloud, how good
He is, how great should be;
Enlargèd winds that curl the flood,
Know no such liberty.

Stone walls do not a prison make,
Nor iron bars a cage;
Mindes innocent and quiet take
That for an hermitage;
If I have freedom in my love,
And in my soul am free;
Angels alone that soar above,
Enjoy such liberty.

RICHARD LOVELACE

A Red, Red Rose

O my luve's like a red, red rose.
That's newly sprung in June;
O my luve's like a melodie
That's sweetly play'd in tune.
As fair art thou, my bonie lass,
So deep in luve am I;
And I will love thee still, my Dear,
Till a' the seas gang dry.
Till a' the seas gang dry, my Dear,
And the rocks melt wi' the sun:
I will luve thee still, my Dear,
While the sands o' life shall run.
And fare thee weel my only Luve!
And fare thee weel a while!
And I will come again, my Luve,
Tho' it were ten thousand mile!

ROBERT BURNS

The Rover

A weary lot is thine, fair maid,
A weary lot is thine!
To pull the thorn thy brow to braid,
And press the rue for wine.
A lightsome eye, a soldier's mien
A feather of the blue,
A doublet of the Lincoln green –
No more of me you knew
My Love!
No more of me you knew.

'This morn is merry June, I trow,
The rose is budding fain;
But she shall bloom in winter snow
Ere we two meet again.'
He turn'd his charger as he spake
Upon the river shore,
He gave the bridle-reins a shake,
Said 'Adieu for evermore.
My Love!
And adieu for evermore.'

SIR WALTER SCOTT

Absence

'Tis not the loss of love's assurance,
It is not doubting what thou art,
But 'tis the too, too long endurance
Of absence, that afflicts my heart.

The fondest thoughts two hearts can cherish,
When each is lonely doom'd to weep,
Are fruits on desert isles that perish,
Or riches buried in the deep.

What though, untouch'd by jealous madness,
Our bosom's peace may fall to wreck;
Th' undoubting heart, that breaks with sadness,
Is but more slowly doom'd to break.

Absence! is not the soul torn by it
From more than light, or life, or breath?
'Tis Lethe's gloom, but not its quiet, –
The pain without the peace of death.

THOMAS CAMPBELL

She is Far From the Land

She is far from the land, where her young hero sleeps,
And lovers are round her, sighing;
But coldly she turns from their gaze, and weeps,
For her heart in his grave is lying!

She sings the wild song of her dear native plains,
Every note which he lov'd awaking
Ah! little they think, who delight in her strains,
How the heart of the Minstrel is breaking!

He had lov'd for his love, for his country he died,
They were all that to life had entwin'd him,
Nor soon shall the tears of his country be dried,
Nor long will his love stay behind him.

Oh! make her a grave, where the sun-beams rest,
When they promise a glorious morrow;
They'll shine o'er her sleep, like a smile from the West,
From her own lov'd Island of sorrow!

THOMAS MOORE

A Farewell

Oft have I mused, but now at length I find
Why those that die, men say, they do depart:
Depart: a word so gentle to my mind,
Weakly did seem to paint Death's ugly dart.

But now the stars, with their strange course, do bind
Me one to leave, with whom I leave my heart;
I hear a cry of spirits faint and blind,
That parting thus, my chiefest part I part.

Part of my life, the loathed part to me,
Lives to impart my weary clay some breath;
But that good part wherein all comforts be,
Now dead, doth show departure is a death:

Yea, worse than death, death parts both woe and joy,
From joy I part, still living in annoy.

Finding those beams, which I must ever love,
To mar my mind, and with my hurt to please,
I deemed it best, some absence for to prove,

If farther place might further me to ease.
My eyes thence drawn, where lived all their light,
Blinded forthwith in dark despair did lie,
Like to the mole, with want of guiding sight,
Deep plunged in earth, deprived of the sky.

In absence blind, and wearied with that woe,
To greater woes, by presence, I return;
Even as the fly, which to the flame doth go,
Pleased with the light, that his small corse doth burn:

Fair choice I have, either to live or die
A blinded mole, or else a burned fly.

SIR PHILIP SIDNEY

Ae Fond Kiss, and Then We Sever

Ae fond kiss, and then we sever;
Ae fareweel, alas, for ever!
Deep in heart-wrung tears I'll pledge thee,
Warring sighs and groans I'll wage thee.
Who shall say that Fortune grieves him,
While the star of hope she leaves him?
Me, nae cheerful twinkle lights me;
Dark despair around benights me.

I'll ne'er blame my partial fancy,
Naething could resist my Nancy:
But to see her was to love her;
Love but her, and love for ever.
Had we never lov'd sae kindly,
Had we never lov'd sae blindly,
Never met – or never parted,
We had ne'er been broken-hearted.

Fare-thee-weel, thou first and fairest!
Fare-thee-weel, thou best and dearest!
Thine be ilka joy and treasure,
Peace, Enjoyment, Love and Pleasure!
Ae fond kiss, and then we sever!
Ae fareweel, alas, for ever!

Deep in heart-wrung tears I'll pledge thee,
Warring sighs and groans I'll wage thee.

ROBERT BURNS

Sonnet XLIV

If the dull substance of my flesh were thought,
Injurious distance should not stop my way;
For then despite of space I would be brought,
From limits far remote where thou dost stay.
No matter then although my foot did stand
Upon the farthest earth removed from thee;
For nimble thought can jump both sea and land
As soon as think the place where he would be.
But ah! thought kills me that I am not thought,
To leap large lengths of miles when thou art gone,
But that so much of earth and water wrought
I must attend time's leisure with my moan,
Receiving nought by elements so slow
But heavy tears, badges of either's woe.

WILLIAM SHAKESPEARE

Harp Song of the Dane Women

What is a woman that you forsake her,
And the hearth-fire and the home-acre,
To go with the old grey Widow-maker?

She has no house to lay a guest in –
But one chill bed for all to rest in,
That the pale suns and the stray bergs nest in.

She has no strong white arms to fold you,
But the ten-times-fingering weed to hold you –
Out on the rocks where the tide has rolled you.

Yet, when the signs of summer thicken,
And the ice breaks, and the birch-buds quicken,
Yearly you turn from our side, and sicken –

Sicken again for the shouts and the slaughters.
You steal away to the lapping waters,
And look at your ship in her winter quarters.
You forget our mirth, and talk at the tables,
The kine in the shed and the horse in the stables –
To pitch her sides and go over her cables.

Then you drive out where the storm-clouds swallow,
And the sound of your oar-blades, falling hollow.
Is all we have left through the months to follow.

Ah, what is Woman that you forsake her,
And the hearth-fire and the home-acre,
To go with the old grey Widow-maker?

RUDYARD KIPLING

To an Absent Lover

That so much change should come when thou dost go,
Is mystery that I cannot ravel quite.
The very house seems dark as when the light
Of lamps goes out. Each wonted thing doth grow
So altered, that I wander to and fro
Bewildered by the most familiar sight,
And feel like one who rouses in the night
From dream of ecstasy, and cannot know
At first if he be sleeping or awake.
My foolish heart so foolish for thy sake
Hath grown, dear one!
Teach me to be more wise.
I blush for all my foolishness doth lack;
I fear to seem a coward in thine eyes.
Teach me, dear one, – but first thou must come back!

HELEN HUNT JACKSON

A Wife in London

I. The Tragedy
She sits in the tawny vapour
That the City lanes have uprolled,
Behind whose webby fold on fold
Like a waning taper
The street-lamp glimmers cold.

A messenger's knock cracks smartly,
Flashed news is in her hand
Of meaning it dazes to understand
Though shaped so shortly:
He – has fallen – in the far South Land…

II. The Irony
'Tis the morrow; the fog hangs thicker,
The postman nears and goes:
A letter is brought whose lines disclose
By the firelight flicker
His hand, whom the worm now knows:

Fresh – firm – penned in highest feather –
Page-full of his hoped return,
And of home-planned jaunts by brake and burn

In the summer weather,
And of new love that they would learn.

THOMAS HARDY

Sonnet XCVII

How like a winter hath my absence been
From thee, the pleasure of the fleeting year!
What freezings have I felt, what dark days seen!
What old December's bareness every where!
And yet this time removed was summer's time,
The teeming autumn, big with rich increase,
Bearing the wanton burden of the prime,
Like widow'd wombs after their lords' decease:
Yet this abundant issue seem'd to me
But hope of orphans and unfather'd fruit;
For summer and his pleasures wait on thee,
And, thou away, the very birds are mute;
Or, if they sing, 'tis with so dull a cheer
That leaves look pale, dreading the winter's near.

WILLIAM SHAKESPEARE

On Parting

The kiss, dear maid! thy lip has left
Shall never part from mine,
Till happier hours restore the gift
Untainted back to thine.

Thy parting glance, which fondly beams,
An equal love may see:
The tear that from thine eyelid streams
Can weep no change in me.

I ask no pledge to make me blest
In gazing when alone;
Nor one memorial for a breast,
Whose thoughts are all thine own.

Nor need I write – to tell the tale
My pen were doubly weak:
Oh! what can idle words avail,
Unless the heart could speak?

By day or night, in weal or woe,
That heart, no longer free,
Must bear the love it cannot show,
And silent ache for thee.

GEORGE GORDON, LORD BYRON

If You Were Coming in the Fall

If you were coming in the fall,
I'd brush the summer by
With half a smile and half a spurn,
As housewives do a fly.

If I could see you in a year,
I'd wind the months in balls,
And put them each in separate drawers,
Until their time befalls.

If only centuries delayed,
I'd count them on my hand,
Subtracting till my fingers dropped
Into Van Diemen's land.

If certain, when this life was out,
That yours and mine should be,
I'd toss it yonder like a rind,
And taste eternity.

But now, all ignorant of the length
Of time's uncertain wing,
It goads me, like the goblin bee,
That will not state its sting.

EMILY DICKINSON

Jean

Of a' the airts the wind can blaw,
I dearly like the west,
For there the bonie lassie lives,
The lassie I lo'e best:
There's wild woods grow, and rivers row,
And mony a hill between;
But day and night my fancy's flight
Is ever wi' my Jean.

I see her in the dewy flowers,
I see her sweet and fair:
I hear her in the tunefu' birds,
I hear her charm the air:
There's not a bonie flower that springs
By fountain, shaw, or green,
There's not a bonie bird that sings,
But minds me o' my Jean.

ROBERT BURNS

Lost Love

A broken heart cannot, of course, be mended
by words, even the most poignant in the English
language. Only time will do that. However,
poems of lost love can help to soothe the pain
and should be taken, like medicine for the heart,
regularly, and in liberal doses.

Along the Field as We Came By

Along the field as we came by
A year ago, my love and I,
The aspen over stile and stone
Was talking to itself alone.
'Oh who are these that kiss and pass?
A country lover and his lass;
Two lovers looking to be wed;
And time shall put them both to bed,
But she shall lie with earth above,
And he beside another love.'

And sure enough beneath the tree
There walks another love with me,
And overhead the aspen heaves
Its rainy-sounding silver leaves;
And I spell nothing in their stir,
But now perhaps they speak to her,
And plain for her to understand
They talk about a time at hand
When I shall sleep with clover clad,
And she beside another lad.

A. E. HOUSMAN

Grown and Flown

I loved my love from green of Spring
Until sere Autumn's fall;
But now that leaves are withering
How should one love at all?
One heart's too small
For hunger, cold, love, everything.
I loved my love on sunny days
Until late Summer's wane;
But now that frost begins to glaze
How should one love again?
Nay, love and pain
Walk wide apart in diverse ways.
I loved my love – alas to see
That this should be, alas!
I thought that this could scarcely be,
Yet has it come to pass:
Sweet sweet love was,
Now bitter bitter grown to me.

CHRISTINA ROSSETTI

No Tears

Under the blue skies of her native land
She languished and began to fade…
Until surely there flew without a sound
Above me, her young shade.
But there stretches between us an uncrossable line;
In vain my feelings I tried to awaken.
The lips that brought the news were made of stone,
And I listened like a stone, unshaken.
So this is she for whom my soul once burned
In the tense and heavy fire,
Obsessed, exhausted, driven out of my mind
By tenderness and desire!
Where are the torments? Where is love? Alas!
For the unreturning days'
Sweet memory and for the poor credulous
Shade, I find no lament, no tears.

ALEXANDER PUSHKIN

So We'll Go No More A-Roving

So, we'll go no more a-roving
So late into the night,
Though the heart be still as loving,
And the moon be still as bright.

For the sword outwears its sheath,
And the soul wears out the breast,
And the heart must pause to breathe,
And love itself have rest.

Though the night was made for loving,
And the day returns too soon,
Yet we'll go no more a-roving
By the light of the moon.

GEORGE GORDON, LORD BYRON

Love's Pains

This love, I canna' bear it,
It cheats me night and day;
This love, I canna' wear it,
It takes my peace away.

This love, wa' once a flower;
But now it is a thorn –
The joy o' evening hour,
Turn'd to a pain e're morn.

This love, it wa' a bud,
And a secret known to me;
Like a flower within a wood;
Like a nest within a tree.

This love, wrong understood,
Oft' turned my joy to pain;
I tried to throw away the bud,
But the blossom would remain.

JOHN CLARE

When I Was One-and-Twenty

When I was one-and-twenty
I heard a wise man say,
'Give crowns and pounds and guineas
But not your heart away;

Give pearls away and rubies
But keep your fancy free.'
But I was one-and-twenty,
No use to talk to me.

When I was one-and-twenty
I heard him say again,
'The heart out of the bosom
Was never given in vain;
'Tis paid with sighs a plenty
And sold for endless rue.'
And I am two-and-twenty,
And oh, 'tis true, 'tis true.

A. E. HOUSMAN

O That 'Twere Possible

O that 'twere possible
After long grief and pain
To find the arms of my true love
Round me once again!…

A shadow flits before me,
Not thou, but like to thee:
Ah, Christ! that it were possible
For one short hour to see
The souls we loved, that they might tell us
What and where they be!

ALFRED, LORD TENNYSON

From One Who Stays

How empty seems the town now you are gone!
A wilderness of sad streets, where gaunt walls
Hide nothing to desire; sunshine falls
Eery, distorted, as it long had shone
On white, dead faces tombed in halls of stone.
The whir of motors, stricken through with calls
Of playing boys, floats up at intervals;
But all these noises blur to one long moan.
What quest is worth pursuing? And how strange
That other men still go accustomed ways!
I hate their interest in the things they do.
A spectre-horde repeating without change
An old routine. Alone I know the days
Are still-born, and the world stopped, lacking you.

AMY LOWELL

Youth Gone and Beauty Gone if Ever There

Youth gone, and beauty gone if ever there
Dwelt beauty in so poor a face as this;
Youth gone and beauty, what remains of bliss?
I will not bind fresh roses in my hair,
To shame a cheek at best but little fair, –
Leave youth his roses, who can bear a thorn, –
I will not seek for blossoms anywhere,
Except such common flowers as blow with corn.
Youth gone and beauty gone, what doth remain?
The longing of a heart pent up forlorn,
A silent heart whose silence loves and longs;
The silence of a heart which sang its songs
While youth and beauty made a summer morn,
Silence of love that cannot sing again.

CHRISTINA ROSSETTI

Farewell to Love

Since there's no help, come, let us kiss and part,
Nay, I have done, you get no more of me,
And I am glad, yea, glad with all my heart,
That thus so cleanly I myself can free.
Shake hands for ever, cancel all our vows,
And when we meet at any time again
Be it not seen in either of our brows
That we one jot of former love retain.
Now at the last gasp of Love's latest breath,
When, his pulse failing, Passion speechless lies,
When Faith is kneeling by his bed of death,
And Innocence is closing up his eyes,
Now, if thou wouldst, when all have giv'n him over,
From death to life thou might'st him yet recover.

MICHAEL DRAYTON

Annabel Lee

It was many and many a year ago,
In a kingdom by the sea,
That a maiden there lived whom you may know
By the name of ANNABEL LEE;
And this maiden she lived with no other thought
Than to love and be loved by me.

I was a child and she was a child,
In this kingdom by the sea;
But we loved with a love that was more than love –
I and my Annabel Lee;
With a love that the winged seraphs of heaven
Coveted her and me.

And this was the reason that, long ago,
In this kingdom by the sea,
A wind blew out of a cloud, chilling
My beautiful Annabel Lee;
So that her highborn kinsman came
And bore her away from me,
To shut her up in a sepulchre
In this kingdom by the sea.

The angels, not half so happy in heaven,
Went envying her and me –
Yes! – that was the reason (as all men know,
In this kingdom by the sea)
That the wind came out of the cloud by night,
Chilling and killing my Annabel Lee.

But our love it was stronger by far than the love
Of those who were older than we –
Of many far wiser than we –
And neither the angels in heaven above,
Nor the demons down under the sea,
Can ever dissever my soul from the soul
Of the beautiful Annabel Lee.

For the moon never beams without bringing me dreams
Of the beautiful Annabel Lee;
And the stars never rise but I feel the bright eyes
Of the beautiful Annabel Lee;
And so, all the night-tide, I lie down by the side
Of my darling – my darling – my life and my bride,
In the sepulchre there by the sea,
In her tomb by the sounding sea.

EDGAR ALLAN POE

Severed Selves

Two separate divided silences,
Which, brought together, would find loving voice;
Two glances which together would rejoice
In love, now lost like stars beyond dark trees;
Two hands apart whose touch alone gives ease;
Two bosoms which, heart-shrined with mutual flame,
Would, meeting in one clasp, be made the same;
Two souls, the shores wave-mocked of sundering seas: –

Such are we now. Ah! may our hope forecast
Indeed one hour again, when on this stream
Of darkened love once more the light shall gleam?
An hour how slow to come, how quickly past,
Which blooms and fades, and only leaves at last,
Faint as shed flowers, the attenuated dream.

DANTE GABRIEL ROSSETTI

The Apparition

When by thy scorn, O murd'ress, I am dead,
And that thou thinkst thee free
From all solicitation from me,
Then shall my ghost come to thy bed,
And thee, feign'd vestal, in worse arms shall see:
Then thy sick taper will begin to wink,
And he, whose thou art then, being tired before,
Will, if thou stir, or pinch to wake him, think
Thou call'st for more,
And, in false sleep, will from thee shrink:
And then, poor aspen wretch, neglected thou
Bathed in a cold quicksilver sweat wilt lie,
A verier ghost than I.
What I will say, I will not tell thee now,
Lest that preserve thee; and since my love is spent,
I'd rather thou shouldst painfully repent,
Than by my threatenings rest still innocent.

JOHN DONNE

Her Voice

The wild bee reels from bough to bough
With his furry coat and his gauzy wing,
Now in a lily-cup, and now
Setting a jacinth bell a-swing,
In his wandering;
Sit closer love: it was here I trow
I made that vow,

Swore that two lives should be like one
As long as the sea-gull loved the sea,
As long as the sunflower sought the sun, –
It shall be, I said, for eternity
'Twixt you and me!
Dear friend, those times are over and done;
Love's web is spun.

Look upward where the poplar trees
Sway and sway in the summer air,
Here in the valley never a breeze
Scatters the thistledown, but there
Great winds blow fair
From the mighty murmuring mystical seas,
And the wave-lashed leas.

Look upward where the white gull screams,
What does it see that we do not see?
Is that a star? or the lamp that gleams
On some outward voyaging argosy, –
Ah! can it be
We have lived our lives in a land of dreams!
How sad it seems.

Sweet, there is nothing left to say
But this, that love is never lost,
Keen winter stabs the breasts of May
Whose crimson roses burst his frost,
Ships tempest-tossed
Will find a harbour in some bay,
And so we may.

And there is nothing left to do
But to kiss once again, and part,
Nay, there is nothing we should rue,
I have my beauty, – you your Art,
Nay, do not start,
One world was not enough for two
Like me and you.

OSCAR WILDE

Heart, We Will Forget Him!

Heart, we will forget him!
You and I, tonight!
You must forget the warmth he gave,
I will forget the light.

When you have done, pray tell me
That I, my thoughts, may dim;
Haste! lest while you're lagging.
I may remember him!

EMILY DICKINSON

The Hour-Glass

Consider this small dust here running in the glass,
By atoms moved;
Could you believe that this the body was
Of one that loved?
And in his mistress' flame, playing like a fly,

Turned to cinders by her eye:
Yes; and in death, as life, unblessed,
To have it expressed,
Even ashes of lovers find no rest.

BEN JONSON

The Night Has a Thousand Eyes

The Night has a thousand eyes,
And the day but one;
Yet the light of the bright world dies
With the dying sun.

The mind has a thousand eyes,
And the heart but one;
Yet the light of a whole life dies
When love is done.

FRANCIS WILLIAM BOURDILLON

Remembrance

Cold in the earth – and the deep snow piled above thee,
Far, far, removed, cold in the dreary grave!
Have I forgot, my only Love, to love thee,
Severed at last by Time's all-severing wave?

Now, when alone, do my thoughts no longer hover
Over the mountains, on that northern shore,
Resting their wings where heath and fern-leaves cover
Thy noble heart for ever, ever more?

Cold in the earth – and fifteen wild Decembers,
From those brown hills, have melted into spring:
Faithful, indeed, is the spirit that remembers
After such years of change and suffering!

Sweet Love of youth, forgive, if I forget thee,
While the world's tide is bearing me along;
Other desires and other hopes beset me,
Hopes which obscure, but cannot do thee wrong!

No later light has lightened up my heaven,
  No second morn has ever shone for me;
All my life's bliss from thy dear life was given,
  All my life's bliss is in the grave with thee.

But, when the days of golden dreams had perished,
  And even Despair was powerless to destroy;
Then did I learn how existence could be cherished,
  Strengthened, and fed without the aid of joy.

Then did I check the tears of useless passion –
  Weaned my young soul from yearning after thine;
Sternly denied its burning wish to hasten
  Down to that tomb already more than mine.

And, even yet, I dare not let it languish,
  Dare not indulge in memory's rapturous pain;
Once drinking deep of that divinest anguish,
  How could I seek the empty world again?

EMILY BRONTË

Without Her

What of her glass without her? The blank grey
There where the pool is blind of the moon's face.
Her dress without her? The tossed empty space
Of cloud-rack whence the moon has passed away.
Her paths without her? Day's appointed sway
Usurped by desolate night. Her pillowed place
Without her? Tears, ah me! for love's good grace,
And cold forgetfulness of night or day.

What of the heart without her? Nay, poor heart,
Of thee what word remains ere speech be still?
A wayfarer by barren ways and chill,
Steep ways and weary, without her thou art,
Where the long cloud, the long wood's counterpart,
Sheds doubled darkness up the labouring hill.

DANTE GABRIEL ROSSETTI

Sonnet XLII

That thou hast her, it is not all my grief,
And yet it may be said I loved her dearly;
That she hath thee is of my wailing chief,
A loss in love that touches me more nearly.
Loving offenders, thus I will excuse ye:
Thou dost love her because thou know'st I love her,
And for my sake even so doth she abuse me,
Suff'ring my friend for my sake to approve her.
If I lose thee, my loss is my love's gain,
And, losing her, my friend hath found that loss;
Both find each other, and I lose both twain,
And both for my sake lay on me this cross:
But here's the joy: my friend and I are one;
Sweet flattery! Then she loves but me alone.

WILLIAM SHAKESPEARE

The Surrender

My once dear love, hapless that I no more
Must call thee so, the rich affection's store
That fed our hope lies now exhaust and spent,
Like sums of treasure unto bankrupts lent.
We, that did nothing study but the way
To love each other, with which thoughts the day
Rose with delight to us and with them set,
Must learn the hateful art, how to forget.
We that did nothing wish that Heaven would give
Beyond ourselves, nor did desire to live
Beyond that wish, all these now cancel must
As if not writ in faith, but words and dust.
Yet witness those clear vows which lovers make,
Witness the chaste desires that never brake
Into unruly heats; witness that breast
Which in thy bosom anchor'd his whole rest;
'Tis no default in us: I dare acquite
Thy maiden faith, thy purpose fair and white
As thy pure self. Cross planets did envy
Us to each other, and Heaven did untie

Faster than vows could bind. Oh, that the stars,
When lovers meet, should stand opposed in wars!
Since, then, some higher destinies command,
Let us not strive, nor labor to withstand
What is past help. The longest date of grief
Can never yield a hope of our relief;
And though we waste ourselves in moist laments,
Tears may drown us, but not our discontents.
Fold back our arms, take home our fruitless loves,
That must new fortunes try, like turtle doves
Dislodged from their haunts. We must in tears
Unwind a love knit up in many years.
In this last kiss I here surrender thee
Back to thy self, so thou again art free;
Thou in another, sad as that, resend
The truest heart that lover e'er did lend.
Now turn from each. So fare our severed hearts
As the divorced soul from her body parts.

HENRY KING

Even So

So it is, my dear.
All such things touch secret strings
For heavy hearts to hear.
So it is, my dear.
Very like indeed:
Sea and sky, afar, on high,
Sand and strewn seaweed, –
Very like indeed.
But the sea stands spread
As one wall with the flat skies,
Where the lean black craft like flies
Seem well-nigh stagnated,
Soon to drop off dead.
Seemed it so to us
When I was thine and thou wast mine,
And all these things were thus,
But all our world in us?
Could we be so now?
Not if all beneath heaven's pall
Lay dead but I and thou,
Could we be so now!

DANTE GABRIEL ROSSETTI

The Banks O'Doon

Ye flowery banks o' bonie Doon,
How can ye blume sae fair?
How can ye chant, ye little birds,
And I sae fu' o' care?
Thou'll break my heart, thou bonie bird,
That sings upon the bough:
Thou minds me o' the happy days
When my fause Luve was true.
Thou'll break my heart, thou bonie bird,
That sings beside thy mate:
For sae I sat, and sae I sang,
And wi' na o' my fate.
Aft hae I rov'd by bonie Doon
To see the woodbine twine,
And ilka bird sang o' its luve,
And sae did I o' mine.
Wi' lightsome heart I pu'd a rose
Frae aiff its thorny tree,
And my fause luver straw my rose,
But left the thorn wi' me.

ROBERT BURNS

Song: 'Sweetest Love I Do Not Go'

Sweetest love, I do not go,
For weariness of thee,
Nor in hope the world can show
A fitter love for me;
But since that I
At the last must part, 'tis best,
Thus to use myself in jest
By feigned deaths to die.

Yesternight the sun went hence,
And yet is here to-day;
He hath no desire nor sense,
Nor half so short a way;
Then fear not me,
But believe that I shall make
Speedier journeys, since I take
More wings and spurs than he.

O how feeble is man's power,
That if good fortune fall,
Cannot add another hour,
Nor a lost hour recall;

But come bad chance,
And we join to it our strength,
And we teach it art and length,
Itself o'er us to advance.

When thou sigh'st, thou sigh'st not wind,
But sigh'st my soul away;
When thou weep'st, unkindly kind,
My life's blood doth decay.
It cannot be
That thou lovest me as thou say'st,
If in thine my life thou waste,
That art the best of me.

Let not thy divining heart
Forethink me any ill;
Destiny may take thy part,
And may thy fears fulfil.
But think that we
Are but turn'd aside to sleep.
They who one another keep
Alive, ne'er parted be.

JOHN DONNE

I Will Not Let Thee Go

I will not let thee go.
Ends all our month-long love in this?
Can it be summed up so,
Quit in a single kiss?
I will not let thee go.

I will not let thee go.
If thy words' breath could scare thy deeds,
As the soft south can blow
And toss the feathered seeds,
Then might I let thee go.

I will not let thee go.
Had not the great sun seen, I might;
Or were he reckoned slow
To bring the false to light,
Then might I let thee go.

I will not let thee go.
The stars that crowd the summer skies
Have watched us so below
With all their million eyes,
I dare not let thee go.

I will not let thee go.
Have we chid the changeful moon,
Now rising late, and now
Because she set too soon,
And shall I let thee go?

I will not let thee go.
Have not the young flowers been content,
Plucked ere their buds could blow,
To seal our sacrament?
I cannot let thee go.

I will not let thee go.
I hold thee by too many bands:
Thou sayest farewell, and lo!
I have thee by the hands,
And will not let thee go.

ROBERT BRIDGES

The Lost Mistress

All's over, then: does truth sound bitter
As one at first believes?
Hark, 'tis the sparrows' good-night twitter
About your cottage eaves!

And the leaf-buds on the vine are woolly,
I noticed that, to-day;
One day more bursts them open fully
– You know the red turns gray.

To-morrow we meet the same then, dearest?
May I take your hand in mine?
Mere friends are we, – well, friends the merest
Keep much that I resign:

For each glance of the eye so bright and black,
Though I keep with heart's endeavour, –
Your voice, when you wish the snowdrops back,
Though it stay in my soul for ever! –

Yet I will but say what mere friends say,
Or only a thought stronger;
I will hold your hand but as long as all may,
Or so very little longer!

ROBERT BROWNING

To the Willow-tree

Thou art to all lost love the best,
The only true plant found,
Wherewith young men and maids distrest,
And left of love, are crown'd.

When once the lover's rose is dead,
Or laid aside forlorn:
Then willow-garlands 'bout the head
Bedew'd with tears are worn.

When with neglect, the lovers' bane,
Poor maids rewarded be
For their love lost, their only gain
Is but a wreath from thee.

And underneath thy cooling shade,
When weary of the light,
The love-spent youth and love-sick maid
Come to weep out the night.

ROBERT HERRICK

Inconstancy Reproved

I do confess thou'rt smooth and fair
And I might have gone near to love thee,
Had I not found the slightest prayer
That lips could move, had power to move thee;
But I can let thee now alone
As worthy to be loved by none.
I do confess thou'rt sweet; yet find
Thee such an unthrift of thy sweets,
Thy favours are but like the wind
That kisseth everything it meets:
And since thou canst with more than one,
Thou'rt worthy to be kissed by none.
The morning rose that untouched stands
Armed with her briers, how sweet she smells!
But plucked and strained through ruder hands,
Her sweets no longer with her dwells:
But scent and beauty both are gone,
And leaves fall from her, one by one.
Such fate ere long will thee betide
When thou hast handled been awhile,
With sere flowers to be thrown aside;

And I shall sigh, while some will smile,
To see thy love to every one
Hath brought thee to be loved by none.

SIR ROBERT AYTON

False Though She Be

False though she be to me and love,
I'll ne'er pursue revenge;
For still the charmer I approve,
Though I deplore her change.

In hours of bliss we oft have met:
They could not always last;
And though the present I regret,
I'm grateful for the past.

WILLIAM CONGREVE

A Farewell to False Love

Farewell, false love, the oracle of lies,
A mortal foe and enemy to rest,
An envious boy, from whom all cares arise,
A bastard vile, a beast with rage possessed,
A way of error, a temple full of treason,
In all effects contrary unto reason.

A poisoned serpent covered all with flowers,
Mother of sighs, and murderer of repose,
A sea of sorrows whence are drawn such showers
As moisture lend to every grief that grows;
A school of guile, a net of deep deceit,
A gilded hook that holds a poisoned bait.

A fortress foiled, which reason did defend,
A siren song, a fever of the mind,
A maze wherein affection finds no end,
A raging cloud that runs before the wind,
A substance like the shadow of the sun,

A goal of grief for which the wisest run.
A quenchless fire, a nurse of trembling fear,
A path that leads to peril and mishap,
A true retreat of sorrow and despair,
An idle boy that sleeps in pleasure's lap,
A deep mistrust of that which certain seems,
A hope of that which reason doubtful deems.

Sith then thy trains my younger years betrayed,
And for my faith ingratitude I find;
And sith repentance hath my wrongs bewrayed,
Whose course was ever contrary to kind:
False love, desire, and beauty frail, adieu.
Dead is the root whence all these fancies grew.

SIR WALTER RALEIGH

Jeanie With the Light Brown Hair

I dream of Jeanie with the light brown hair,
Borne, like a vapor, on the summer air;
I see her tripping where the bright streams play,
Happy as the daisies that dance on her way.
Many were the wild notes her merry voice would pour.
Many were the blithe birds that warbled them o'er:
Oh! I dream of Jeanie with the light brown hair,
Floating, like a vapor, on the soft summer air.

I long for Jeanie with the daydawn smile,
Radiant in gladness, warm with winning guile;
I hear her melodies, like joys gone by,
Sighing round my heart o'er the fond hopes that die: –
Sighing like the night wind and sobbing like the rain, –
Wailing for the lost one that comes not again:
Oh! I long for Jeanie, and my heart bows low,
Never more to find her where the bright waters flow.

I sigh for Jeanie, but her light form strayed
Far from the fond hearts round her native glade;
Her smiles have vanished and her sweet songs flown,
Flitting like the dreams that have cheered us and gone.

Now the nodding wild flowers may wither on the shore
While her gentle fingers will cull them no more:
Oh! I sigh for Jeanie with the light brown hair,
Floating, like a vapor, on the soft summer air.

STEPHEN FOSTER

To ——
('*When I Loved You, I Can't But Allow*')

When I loved you, I can't but allow
I had many an exquisite minute:
But the scorn that I feel for you now
Hath even more luxury in it!

Thus, whether we're on or we're off,
Some witchery seems to await you;
To love you is pleasant enough,
And, oh! 'tis delicious to hate you!

THOMAS MOORE

To My Inconstant Mistress

When thou, poor excommunicate
From all the joys of love, shalt see
The full reward and glorious fate
Which my strong faith shall purchase me,
Then curse thine own inconstancy.

A fairer hand than thine shall cure
That heart, which thy false oaths did wound;
And to my soul, a soul more pure
Than thine shall by Love's hand be bound,
And both with equal glory crown'd.

Then shalt thou weep, entreat, complain
To Love, as I did once to thee;
When all thy tears shall be as vain
As mine were then, for thou shalt be
Damn'd for thy false apostasy.

THOMAS CAREW

A Complaint

There is a change – and I am poor;
Your love hath been, nor long ago,
A fountain at my fond heart's door,
Whose only business was to flow;
And flow it did; not taking heed
Of its own bounty, or my need.

What happy moments did I count!
Blest was I then all bliss above!
Now, for that consecrated fount
Of murmuring, sparkling, living love,
What have I? Shall I dare to tell?
A comfortless and hidden well.

A well of love – it may be deep –
I trust it is, – and never dry:
What matter? If the waters sleep
In silence and obscurity.
– Such change, and at the very door
Of my fond heart, hath made me poor.

WILLIAM WORDSWORTH

The Going

Why did you give no hint that night
That quickly after the morrow's dawn,
And calmly, as if indifferent quite,
You would close your term here, up and be gone
Where I could not follow
With wing of swallow
To gain one glimpse of you ever anon!

Never to bid good-bye,
Or lip me the softest call,
Or utter a wish for a word, while I
Saw morning harden upon the wall,
Unmoved, unknowing
That your great going
Had place that moment, and altered all.

Why do you make me leave the house
And think for a breath it is you I see
At the end of the alley of bending boughs
Where so often at dusk you used to be;
Till in darkening dankness
The yawning blankness
Of the perspective sickens me!

You were she who abode
By those red-veined rocks far West,
You were the swan-necked one who rode
Along the beetling Beeny Crest,
And, reining nigh me,
Would muse and eye me,
While Life unrolled us its very best.

Why, then, latterly did we not speak,
Did we not think of those days long dead,
And ere your vanishing strive to seek
That time's renewal? We might have said,
'In this bright spring weather
We'll visit together
Those places that once we visited.'

Well, well! All's past amend,
Unchangeable. It must go.
I seem but a dead man held on end
To sink down soon… O you could not know
That such swift fleeing
No soul foreseeing –
Not even I – would undo me so!

THOMAS HARDY

When the Lamp is Shattered

When the lamp is shattered
The light in the dust lies dead –
When the cloud is scattered
The rainbow's glory is shed.
When the lute is broken,
Sweet tones are remembered not;
When the lips have spoken,
Loved accents are soon forgot.

As music and splendour
Survive not the lamp and the lute,
The heart's echoes render
No song when the spirit is mute: –
No song but sad dirges,
Like the wind through a ruined cell,
Or the mournful surges
That ring the dead seaman's knell.

When hearts have once mingled
Love first leaves the well-built nest;
The weak one is singled
To endure what it once possessed.

O Love! who bewailest
The frailty of all things here,
Why choose you the frailest
For your cradle, your home, and your bier?
Its passions will rock thee
As the storms rock the ravens on high;
Bright reason will mock thee,
Like the sun from a wintry sky.
From thy nest every rafter
Will rot, and thine eagle home
Leave thee naked to laughter,
When leaves fall and cold winds come.

PERCY BYSSHE SHELLEY

Desideria

Surprised by joy – impatient as the Wind
I turned to share the transport – O! with whom
But Thee, deep buried in the silent tomb,
That spot which no vicissitude can find?
Love, faithful love, recall'd thee to my mind –
But how could I forget thee? Through what power,
Even for the least division of an hour,
Have I been so beguiled as to be blind
To my most grievous loss? – That thought's return
Was the worst pang that sorrow ever bore,
Save one, one only, when I stood forlorn,
Knowing my heart's best treasure was no more;
That neither present time, nor years unborn
Could to my sight that heavenly face restore.

WILLIAM WORDSWORTH

At the Mid Hour of Night

At the mid hour of night, when stars are weeping, I fly
To the lone vale we lov'd, when life shone warm in thine eye;
And I think that, if spirits can steal from the regions of air,
To visit past scenes of delight, thou wilt come to me there,
And tell me our love is remember'd, ev'n in the sky.

Then I sing the wild song, which once 'twas rapture to hear
When our voices both mingling, breath'd like one on the ear;
And, as echo far off through the vale my sad orison rolls,
I think, oh my love! 'tis thy voice from the kingdom of souls
Faintly answering still the notes that once were so dear.

THOMAS MOORE

The Appeal

And wilt thou leave me thus!
Say nay! say nay! for shame!
To save thee from the blame
Of all my grief and grame.
And wilt thou leave me thus?
 Say nay! say nay!

And wilt thou leave me thus,
That hath loved thee so long
In wealth and woe among:
And is thy heart so strong
As for to leave me thus?
 Say nay! say nay!

And wilt thou leave me thus,
That hath given thee my heart
Never for to depart
Neither for pain nor smart:
And wilt thou leave me thus?
 Say nay! say nay!

And wilt thou leave me thus,
And have no more pity
Of him that loveth thee?
Alas! thy cruelty!

And wilt thou leave me thus?
Say nay! say nay!

SIR THOMAS WYATT

An Epitaph Upon Husband and Wife

To these whom death again did wed
This grave's the second marriage-bed.
For though the hand of Fate could force
'Twixt soul and body a divorce,
It could not sever man and wife,
Because they both lived but one life.
Peace, good reader, do not weep;
Peace, the lovers are asleep.
They, sweet turtles, folded lie
In the last knot that love could tie.
Let them sleep, let them sleep on,
Till the stormy night be gone,
And the eternal morrow dawn;
Then the curtains will be drawn,
And they wake into a light
Whose day shall never die in night.

RICHARD CRASHAW

Where Shall the Lover Rest

Where shall the lover rest
Whom the fates sever
From his true maiden's breast
Parted for ever?
Where, through groves deep and high
Sounds the far billow,
Where early violets die
Under the willow.
Eleu loro
Soft shall be his pillow.

There through the summer day
Cool streams are laving;
There, while the tempests sway,
Scarce are boughs waving;
There thy rest shalt thou take,
Parted for ever,
Never again to wake,
Never, O never!
Eleu loro
Never, O never!

Where shall the traitor rest,
He, the deceiver,
Who could win maiden's breast,
Ruin, and leave her?
In the lost battle,
Borne down by the flying,
Where mingles war's rattle
With groans of the dying;
Eleu loro
There shall he be lying.

Her wing shall the eagle flap
O'er the falsehearted;
His warm blood the wolf shall lap
Ere life be parted:
Shame and dishonour sit
By his grave ever;
Blessing shall hallow it
Never, O never!
Eleu loro
Never, O never!

SIR WALTER SCOTT

Farewell Love

Farewell, Love, and all thy laws for ever:
Thy baited hooks shall tangle me no more.
Senec and Plato call me from thy lore,
To perfect wealth my wit for to endeavour.
In blind error when I did persever,
Thy sharp repulse, that pricketh aye so sore,
Hath taught me to set in trifles no store,
And scape forth, since liberty is lever.
Therefore farewell, go trouble younger hearts,
And in me claim no more authority;
With idle youth go use thy property,
And thereon spend thy many brittle darts.
For, hitherto though I've lost my time,
Me lusteth no longer rotten boughs to climb.

SIR THOMAS WYATT

Remember

Remember me when I am gone away,
   Gone far away into the silent land;
When you can no more hold me by the hand,
   Nor I half turn to go, yet turning stay.
Remember me when no more day by day
   You tell me of our future that you plann'd:
   Only remember me; you understand
   It will be late to counsel then or pray.
   Yet if you should forget me for a while
And afterwards remember, do not grieve:
For if the darkness and corruption leave
   A vestige of the thoughts that once I had,
Better by far you should forget and smile
Than that you should remember and be sad.

CHRISTINA ROSSETTI

Biographies

Eliza Acton (1799–1859). Born in Battle in Sussex, Eliza Acton was a poet and cook who wrote one of Britain's first cookbooks aimed at amateur chefs – *Modern Cookery for Private Families* (1845). Her first volume of poetry, *Poems*, was published in 1826 following a stay in France. She went on to publish single, longer poems.

Dante Alighieri (c.1265–1321). Born into a prominent Florentine family, Dante was arguably the greatest Italian poet of the Middle Ages. His *Divine Comedy*, written between 1307 and 1321, is recognized as one of the greatest works of Italian literature. He is sometimes described as 'the father of the Italian language'.

Elizabeth Akers Allen (1832–1911). The American author, journalist and poet Elizabeth Akers Allen began writing poetry at the age of 15 under the pseudonym Florence Percy. She travelled in Europe, reporting for American newspapers and married Paul Akers, a sculptor she met in Rome. She published her first volume of poetry in 1855 and a number of others followed.

Matthew Arnold (1822–88). Arnold was employed for thirty-five years as an inspector of schools in addition to his work as a poet and cultural critic. His poetry was written between 1845 and 1867 after which, believing himself no longer capable of conveying joy, he published only prose. He was elected Professor of Poetry at Oxford University in 1858.

Alfred Austin (1835–1913). Born near Leeds, Alfred Austin became a barrister in 1857 before devoting his life to literature. He edited the *National Review* and wrote for the *Evening Standard*. He was appointed Poet Laureate in 1896 after the death of Alfred, Lord Tennyson.

Sir Robert Ayton (1570–1638). Sir Robert Ayton was a Scottish poet and courtier who was at one time Ambassador to the Holy Roman

Emperor. Written in English, not Scots, his extant poems are few in number but of great quality. Robert Burns admired his work and Ayton's poem *Old Long Syne* is thought to have influenced Burns' *Auld Lang Syne*. He is buried in Westminster Abbey.

Aphra Behn (1640?–89). Aphra Behn was one of the first women to earn a living from writing. Reportedly bisexual, she visited Surinam when young, returning to England in 1664 and marrying a Dutch merchant, Johan Behn, who died a few years later. She later became a spy for Charles II in Antwerp and is buried in Westminster Abbey.

William Blake (1757–1827). William Blake saw himself as a visionary. He was born in London and studied art at the Royal Academy. He published numerous volumes of unconventional poetry, illustrating them with his own brilliant etchings until the 1820s. Late in his life he devoted himself to pictorial art.

Francis William Bourdillon (1852–1921). English poet and translator Francis William Bourdillon was educated at Oxford. He was tutor to the sons of Prince Christian of Schleswig-Holstein and later tutored for the University of Eastbourne. He published several volumes of poetry as well as translations and wrote a novel, *Nephelé*.

Anne Bradstreet (*c.*1612–72). Anne Bradstreet emigrated to America from her native Northampton in 1630 with her husband, Simon Bradstreet, who would become governor of the Massachusetts Bay Colony. She had eight children and a volume of her poetry, *The Tenth Muse Lately Sprung Up in America*, was published in 1850.

Christopher Brennan (1870–1932). Australian poet and scholar Christopher Brennan was born in Sydney, the son of a brewer. He became a library cataloguer and in 1914 published his major work, *Poems: 1913*. He was devastated by the death of his lover Violet Singer and, after losing his job due to increasing drunkenness, he died in poverty.

Robert Bridges OM (1844–1930). Robert Bridges was Poet Laureate from 1913 until 1930. He was born in Kent and educated at Eton and Oxford. He became a doctor but was forced to retire through ill health aged 38 and devoted the remainder of his life to poetry and literary research.

Emily Brontë (1818–48). Born at Haworth on the North Yorkshire moors, Emily Brontë, author of *Wuthering Heights*, was the sister of the novelists Charlotte and Anne. Her first volume of poetry, published in 1846, was written under a male pseudonym. Her poetry is characterized by a brooding mysticism and an attempt to transcend the bleak, physical world.

Rupert Brooke (1887–1915). Educated at Rugby and Cambridge University, Rupert Brooke enlisted in the British army at the outbreak of the First World War, dying a year later of dysentery on a troopship bound for Gallipoli. His war poetry is much loved, especially the immortal lines in *The Soldier: If I should die, think only this of me:/ That there is some corner of a foreign field/ That is for ever England.*

Elizabeth Barrett Browning (1806–61). An unusually well-educated woman for her time, Elizabeth Barrett Browning eloped to Italy in 1846 with fellow poet Robert Browning. An invalid for much of her life, Italy reinvigorated her. Best known for her *Sonnets from the Portuguese* – a sequence of 44 love poems to her husband – her reputation was far greater than his by the end of her life.

Robert Browning (1812–89). Born in London and educated at London University, Robert Browning's reputation was made by the publication of *Dramatis Personae* in 1861 and the very popular *The Ring and the Book* three years later. He had written drama when young and this skill informed his brilliant and refreshing dramatic monologues which used conversational language instead of conventional poetic diction.

Robert Burns (1759–96). The national poet of Scotland, Robert Burns was born into a farming family in Ayrshire and was largely self-taught. His first book, *Poems, Chiefly in the Scottish Dialect* (1786) proved a success but he returned home from Edinburgh to farm and work as an excise-man. He mostly wrote in Scots, is viewed as a pioneer of Romanticism and is recognized as an influence on the founders of liberalism and socialism.

George Gordon, Lord Byron (1788–1824). Born in Aberdeen, Byron became an overnight sensation with the publication of his first volume of poetry in 1812. Following a notorious affair with his half-sister he left England, first spending time in Switzerland and Italy with the poet Shelley, before fighting for independence in Greece where he died, becoming a Greek national hero in the process.

Thomas Campbell (1777–1844). Thomas Campbell was born, the youngest of eleven children, in Glasgow and fame arrived with the 1799 publication of *The Pleasures of Hope*. In 1819 he published his important critical survey – *Specimens of the British Poets* but he is mainly remembered for lyrical war poems such as *Ye Mariners of England* and *Hohenlinden*.

Thomas Carew (1598?–1639?). After a number of positions as secretary to ambassadors in Venice, The Hague and France, Carew (pronounced 'Carey') was made a gentleman of the privy chamber by Charles I in 1628. He was a member of the group that included his associates, Sir John Suckling and Richard Lovelace, known as the 'Cavalier' poets.

William Cartwright (1611–43). Dramatist and clergyman William Cartwright was born in Gloucestershire. His dramatic work was reminiscent of Ben Jonson's comedic style. His collected poems (1651) contains verses in praise of him by Henry Lawes, Izaak Walton and Henry Vaughan among others and the King wore mourning on the day of his funeral.

Alice Cary (1820–71). Self-taught American poet Alice Cary was born near Cincinnati into a farming family. She and her sister Phoebe began writing poetry at the age of 17, the *Poems of Alice and Phoebe Cary* (1849) making the sisters famous. They moved to New York where they continued writing and hosted Sunday evening receptions for the great and the good.

Catullus (*c.*84 BC–*c.*54 BC). Catullus was born into a prominent Verona family and his father was a friend of Julius Caesar. After a time in Rome, in 57 BC he went to Bithynia to work for the governor of the eastern province before returning to Rome where he lived for the remainder of his life. His most memorable poems are about 'Lesbia', thought to be the aristocratic Clodia, wife of the Consul Metellus Celer.

George Chapman (*c.*1559–1634). Poet, dramatist and translator George Chapman is best known for his 1624 translations of Homer, as immortalized by John Keats in his poem *On First Looking Into Chapman's Homer*. Born in Hitchin, he was self-taught and spent several years in military service in Europe. Later in life he led an impecunious existence and was imprisoned for debt.

John Clare (1793–1864). The 'ploughman poet' John Clare was born in the tiny village of Helpstone in Northamptonshire, leaving school at 12 to work in a variety of agricultural jobs. His first book of poems was a roaring success although his later volumes were less successful. After showing symptoms of mental illness for a number of years, he ended his days in Northampton General Asylum.

Hartley Coleridge (1796–1849). Hartley Coleridge was born in Bristol and was the eldest son of poet Samuel Taylor Coleridge. He studied at Oxford and inherited much of his father's character – both the good and the bad points. He spent two years in London writing short poems for the *London Magazine* before becoming a partner in a school at Ambleside, a scheme which failed miserably. His literary reputation chiefly rests on his sonnets and an unfinished lyric drama, *Prometheus*.

Samuel Taylor Coleridge (1772–1834). Born in Devon and raised in London, Coleridge fell into a dissolute lifestyle while studying at Cambridge. In 1798 he published, with the help of William Wordsworth, the important *Lyrical Ballads* described as 'one of the most revolutionary collections of poetry in the history of English literature.' He became addicted to opium and is remembered for poems such as *Kubla Khan* and *The Rime of the Ancient Mariner*.

William Congreve (1670–1729). Born in West Yorkshire, Congreve spent his childhood in Ireland, meeting Jonathan Swift during his time at Trinity College, Dublin. He studied law but became a playwright, writing some of the most popular plays of the Restoration period.

Henry Constable (1562–1613). Poet and spy Henry Constable was educated at Cambridge before becoming a Catholic and moving to Paris where he became an agent for King Henri IV. He carried out confidential missions to both England and Scotland. He was imprisoned in the Tower of London in 1604, but released the same year. His first publication came in 1592 with a collection of 22 sonnets entitled *Diana*.

Eliza Cook (1818–89). Eliza Cook, a Chartist poet and author, and fervent advocate of sexual and political freedom for women, was born in Southwark in London. She contributed to magazines from an early age and published collections of poetry in 1838, 1864 and 1865. Her poem *The Old Armchair* made her a household name in Britain and America.

George Crabbe (1754–1832). George Crabbe was born in poverty in Aldeburgh in Suffolk where he would later become parish doctor before taking up a literary career in London in 1780. He joined the clergy, becoming curate of Aldeburgh in 1871. In 1783, he produced *The Village*, a grimly realistic poetic depiction of rural life.

Hart Crane (1899–1932). Born in Ohio, Crane moved to New York where he worked as an advertising copywriter, before sailing to Mexico to write an epic about the Spanish Conquest. On the return trip to New York he committed suicide by throwing himself into shark-infested waters. His best work can be found in *The Bridge*, his 'mythical synthesis of America'.

Stephen Crane (1871–1900). Stephen Crane earned fame and fortune with his second novel, the American Civil War narrative *The Red Badge of Courage*. He was born in Newark, New Jersey and was better known for his prose than his poetry. His poetry was innovative for its time and consequently it was badly received.

Richard Crashaw (1613–49). His mother and stepmother having died before he was nine, Crashaw's youth was spent rebelling against his father, a Puritan preacher. When the Royalists were defeated by Cromwell, he went into exile for two years and converted to Catholicism. He found work as an assistant to an Italian cardinal and then as sub-canon at the Cathedral of Loretto. His *Steps to the Temple, Sacred Poems* and *Other Delights of the Muses* (1646) contains both religious and secular poems.

Emily Dickinson (1830–86). Born into a prominent family at Amherst, Massachusetts, Emily Dickinson lived most of her uneventful life there, rarely venturing out due to agoraphobia. No more than a dozen of her poems were published during her lifetime, although she wrote almost 2,000 filled with characteristic irony, scepticism and sardonic wit.

John Donne (1572–1631). Son of a London ironmonger, John Donne studied at Oxford before taking part in a naval expedition against Spain in 1595 and voyaging to the Azores in 1596. His career as a courtier ended abruptly when his secret marriage to 17-year-old Anne More, niece of Sir Thomas Egerton, Lord Keeper of the Grand Seal, was discovered. He entered the Church instead and in 1621 become Dean of St. Paul's Cathedral. Although very few of his poems were published in his lifetime, they circulated widely in manuscript form.

William Douglas (1672?–1748). Douglas was a captain in the Royal Scots, fighting in Germany and Spain. He fell in love with Anna or Annie Laurie, youngest daughter of Robert Laurie of Maxwelton, but her father forbade her from marrying him, possibly because of his Jacobite allegiance. Douglas married another and was forced into exile because of his political beliefs. He became a mercenary.

Michael Drayton (1563–1631). Michael Drayton was born in Warwickshire and brought up as a page at the home of Sir Henry

Goodyere whose daughter Anne he was in love with for many years. He decided to become a poet at the age of 10 and even without the benefit of a university education, mastered all the renaissance poetic styles.

John Dryden (1631–1700). Dryden, the son of a country gentleman, attended Westminster School and Trinity College, Cambridge. He welcomed the Restoration of Charles II and remained a Royalist for the remainder of his life, becoming Poet Laureate in 1668 and converting to Catholicism in his later years. On the accession of William and Mary in 1688, he lost his public offices and supported himself by writing plays and translating.

George Eliot (1819–80). George Eliot is the pen-name of Mary Anne Evans who was better known as the writer of novels such as *Middlemarch, Adam Bede* and *The Mill on the Floss.* Her first novel was published in 1859 and she continued writing popular novels for the next fifteen years, distancing herself with a masculine name from the generally light novels of many female novelists of the time.

Anne Finch, Countess of Winchilsea (1661–1720). Born in Sydmonton, Berkshire, Anne Finch met her future husband, Colonel Heneage Finch, at court while serving as a maid of honour to the future wife of James II. Encouraged by her husband, she began to write in the 1680s but her long poem *The Spleen*, published in 1701, was one of the few of her poems to be published in her lifetime.

John Fletcher (1579–1625). John Fletcher, son of the Bishop of London, was born at Rye in Sussex and studied at Cambridge. He befriended Francis Beaumont and co-wrote a number of plays with him. The pair became, alongside Shakespeare, leading writers for the theatre company the King's Men.

Thomas Ford (*c.*1580–1648). Little is known about the composer, lutenist, viol player and poet, Thomas Ford, apart from the fact that he was musician to Henry, Prince of Wales, and occupied the same position at the court of Charles I from 1626 until the outbreak of the English Civil War.

Mary Weston Fordham (*c*.1862-?). Everything that is known about the African-American poet Mary Weston Fordham comes from the poems in her only collection, *Magnolia Leaves* (1897) for which anti-slavery activist Booker T. Washington wrote the introduction. She is thought to have originated from South Carolina.

Stephen Foster (1826–64). The 'Father of American Music' Stephen Foster was born in Lawrenceville, Pennsylvania and, even though he had no formal musical training, wrote some of 19th-century America's favourite music – *Oh! Susanna, Camptown Races, My Old Kentucky Home, Swanee River* and *Jeanie With the Light Brown Hair*. He earned little money, however, dying destitute at the age of 37.

Benjamin Franklin (1706–90). Benjamin Franklin was one of America's Founding Fathers. An author, printer, satirist, politician, scientist, inventor, statesman and diplomat, he was one of the Enlightenment's major figures, making notable achievements in every field in which he was involved.

Khalil Gibran (1883–1931). Khalil Gibran was born in Bsharri in what would become Lebanon. While still a young man, his family moved to the United States where he studied art and began to write. He is known for his book of inspirational poetic essays, *The Prophet*, published in 1923, which became one of the United States' bestselling books of the 20th century.

Johann Wolfgang von Goethe (1749–1832). Born in Frankfurt, Goethe is universally recognized as Germany's greatest man of letters. He was a true polymath, his output embracing poetry, drama, theology, philosophy, humanism and science. While practising law at Weimar, in 1772 he published the novel *The Sorrows of Young Werther* which brought him worldwide fame, if not wealth. His influence was widespread during the coming century in the fields of poetry, music, drama and philosophy.

Gerald Griffin (1803–40). Irish novelist, poet and playwright Gerald Griffin was born in Limerick in Ireland, the son of a brewer. In 1823 he moved to London to become a journalist, later turning to fiction. However, in 1838 he took the drastic decision to burn all his manuscripts before joining a Catholic religious order.

Thomas Hardy (1840–1928). Born in Dorset, Thomas Hardy was apprenticed to an architect at 16. He considered taking holy orders, but lost his faith and returned to Dorset from London to become one of English literature's best-loved novelists with novels such as *Tess of the D'Urbervilles, Jude the Obscure* and *Far From the Madding Crowd*. He began writing poetry in 1897, dedicating the last 30 years of his life to it.

Sir John Harrington (1561–1612). Courtier, author and master of art, Sir John Harrington was the godson of Queen Elizabeth I and a prominent member of her court until his poetry and other writings put him out of favour. He is also, famously, the inventor of the flushing toilet.

Heinrich Heine (1797–1856). Heinrich Heine was the greatest of the German Romantic poets, as well as a journalist and essayist. Born in Düsseldorf, he proved unsuccessful as a businessman, taking up law instead. However, his Jewishness prevented him from entering the profession and he converted to Lutheranism. He lived in Paris for the last 25 years of his life.

Robert Herrick (1591–1674). Born into a family of wealthy London goldsmiths, Herrick studied at Cambridge before returning to London where he became a friend of Ben Jonson. He entered the clergy and was chaplain on the Duke of Buckingham's disastrous expedition to the Île de Ré in 1627. During many years in Devon he wrote more than 2,500 poems, many written to imaginary mistresses.

Thomas Hood (1799–1845). Thomas Hood was born in London, the son of a bookseller. He worked in a counting house before studying engraving which he used to illustrate his work as a humorist, the work for which he was best known during his lifetime.

Gerard Manley Hopkins (1844–89). Under the influence of Cardinal John Henry Newman, Stratford-born and Oxford-educated Hopkins converted to Catholicism in 1866, entering the Society of Jesuits in 1868. Ordained in 1877, he became a parish priest and classics teacher. He stopped writing poetry in 1868 believing that it interfered with his duties but his fellow Jesuits encouraged him to resume and he did so in 1875. Little of his work was published in his lifetime.

A. E. Housman (1859–1936). Born in Worcestershire and educated at Oxford, Alfred Edward Housman worked for ten years in the Patent Office while studying and writing in his spare time. *A Shropshire Lad*, his first collection of poetry was self-published in 1896. An avowed classicist, he was appointed Professor of Latin at Trinity College, Cambridge in 1911.

Henry Howard, Earl of Surrey (*c*.1517–47). Writer of courtly poems and translator of Petrarch's sonnets, Henry Howard fought in battles against the French and was first imprisoned in 1537 on suspicion of participating in a rebellion against the dissolution of the monasteries. Two of Henry VIII's wives were his nieces. He was executed for treason at the age of 30.

James Leigh Hunt (1784–1859). Critic, essayist, writer and poet, James Henry Leigh Hunt was born in London, the son of a popular preacher. He published his first volume of poetry in 1801, wrote for newspapers and in 1807 published a book of theatre criticism. He worked at the War Office before becoming a magazine editor, one article critical of the Prince Regent resulted in two years' imprisonment. He was a close friend of Keats, Byron and Shelley.

Helen Hunt Jackson (1830–85). Born Helen Fiske in Amherst, Massachusetts, where she was a classmate of Emily Dickinson, Helen Hunt Jackson is best remembered as the author of *Ramona*, a novel about the treatment of Native Americans in Southern California.

Ben Jonson (1572–1637). Born in London, Ben Jonson worked as a bricklayer before enlisting in the army. He then became an actor and a playwright and after killing a fellow actor in a duel, narrowly escaped hanging. After finding royal disfavour for his plays he eventually became a favourite of James I. He was the author of numerous successful plays including *Volpone, The Alchemist* and *Bartholomew Fair* and was the first English poet to inspire a 'school', its members including Robert Herrick and Thomas Carew.

John Keats (1795–1821). John Keats trained to be a doctor in London before abandoning medicine for poetry. In 1818 he fell in love with Fanny Brawne but could not afford to marry her. In 1819, known as his *annus mirabilis*, he produced much of his great work – the odes, sonnets and other poems. In 1820 he developed tuberculosis and he died in Rome the following spring, aged 25.

Henry King (1592–1669). Son of the Bishop of London, Henry King entered the clergy and in 1642 became Bishop of Chichester. Removed from his position by the Parliamentarians, he was reinstated in 1660 when Charles II took the throne. He composed both secular and religious poetry and in 1657 published anonymously *Poems, Elegies, Paradoxes* and *Sonnets*.

Rudyard Kipling (1865–1936). Born to British parents in Bombay, Rudyard Kipling was educated in England before returning to India where he worked as a journalist. In 1889 he relocated to England and became famous for his prose. Awarded the Nobel Prize for Literature in 1907, his literary star had waned considerably by the time of his death. Apart from poetry and journalism, Kipling wrote fiction, best-known of which is probably *Jungle Book* (1894) and *Kim* (1901).

Walter Savage Landor (1775–1864). Born in Warwick and educated at Trinity College, Cambridge, Walter Savage Landor lived in Italy from 1815 until 1835 and again from 1857 until his death. A fervent classicist, he was an influence on poets such as Robert Browning and Ezra Pound.

Sidney Lanier (1842–81). Sidney Lanier, born in Macon, Georgia, fought on the Confederate side in the American Civil War and while imprisoned by the Union forces he probably contracted the tuberculosis that eventually killed him. After the war, he was a flutist for the *Peabody Symphony* and lectured in literature at Johns Hopkins University. As well as poetry, he wrote novels.

D. H. Lawrence (1885–1930). David Herbert Lawrence was born in Nottinghamshire and studied at University College, Nottingham. From 1912 he led a nomadic existence, living in Italy, Ceylon, Australia, Mexico, the United States and elsewhere. He is renowned as a novelist, crafting many controversial but acclaimed novels including *Sons and Lovers*, *Women in Love* and *Lady Chatterley's Lover*.

Henry Wadsworth Longfellow (1807–82). Born in Portland, Maine, Henry Wadsworth Longfellow was made Professor of Modern Languages at Bowdoin College where he had obtained his degree. In 1835, he was appointed Professor of Modern Languages at Harvard where he remained until 1854 when he became a full-time writer, works such as *The Song of Hiawatha* making him extremely popular. Longfellow translated poetry and also wrote fiction and verse drama.

Richard Lovelace (1618–58). The 'Cavalier' poet Richard Lovelace was born into a wealthy Kent family. Educated at Charterhouse and Oxford University, he lived the life of a courtier before fighting the Scots in the campaign of 1639–40. He was imprisoned by the Parliamentarians due to his royalist beliefs in 1642 and again in 1648 for fighting for the French. His final years were spent in poverty.

Amy Lowell (1874–1925). Amy Lowell was born into a prominent Brookline, Massachusetts family in which the poet James Russell Lowell was her uncle and another poet, Robert Lowell, was her nephew. Mainly self-taught, from 1914 she lived with the actress Ada Dwyer Russell, the inspiration for many of her poems. She became a leading figure in the poetry movement known as 'Imagism' which led to her poetry moving closer to free verse.

Christopher Marlowe (1564–93). Born in Canterbury, Christopher Marlowe's father was a shoemaker. His years at Corpus Christi College, Cambridge, were spent writing plays and he also worked as a spy abroad. Constantly in trouble and in and out of jail, Marlowe's contacts at court always worked in his favour. He wrote seven plays, including *Edward II* and *Doctor Faustus* and died mysteriously of a knife wound in a tavern brawl aged only 29.

Andrew Marvell (1621–78). A Yorkshireman by birth, Andrew Marvell was educated at Trinity College, Cambridge. During the Civil War, he lived in Europe, returning to befriend literary figures such as John Milton and Richard Lovelace. He was Oliver Cromwell's unofficial laureate and in 1657 replaced Milton as secretary to the Council of State before becoming MP for Hull. Much of his work remained unpublished until after his death.

Alice Meynell (1847–1922). Born in Barnes, in London, Alice Meynell was an editor, critic and suffragist, as well as a poet. She was brought up mainly in Italy and her father was a friend of Charles Dickens. Her first collection of poetry was published in 1875 and, although praised by John Ruskin, did not sell well. She became a prominent figure in the Women Writers' Suffrage League, which was active between 1908 and 1919.

Thomas Moore (1779–1852). The Irish poet, singer, songwriter and entertainer, Thomas Moore, is often considered the national bard of Ireland. Educated at Trinity College, Dublin, he became famous as a balladeer. Relocating to London, he became a well-known society figure and was appointed Registrar to the Admiralty in Bermuda, after which trip he published *Epistles, Odes* and *Other Poems*. In debt, he was forced to leave Britain to live in Paris, becoming literary executor of Lord Byron. He eventually settled at Bromham in England working as a novelist and biographer as well as a successful poet.

William Morris (1834–96). William Morris was responsible for a revival in the decorative arts in Victorian Britain. Born in Walthamstow and educated at Oxford, he trained as an architect, but abandoned that career to design furniture for his own company. He founded the Society for the Preservation of Ancient Buildings and wrote and lectured on socialism.

Edith Nesbit (1858–1924). Edith Nesbit is famous for the numerous children's books – *The Railway Children* amongst them – she published under the name of E. Nesbit. A political activist, she was a founder of the Fabian Society. She was born in London and brought up in Buckinghamshire, France, Spain and Germany.

Coventry Patmore (1823–96). Best known for his poem about a happy marriage, *The Angel in the House*, poet and critic Coventry Patmore was born at Woodford in Essex. Initially an artist, he began to write poetry after spending time at a school in France. He worked for many years as assistant librarian at the British Museum and was a member of the Pre-Raphaelite Brotherhood.

Katherine Philips ('Orinda') (1632–64). The best-known female poet of her age, Katherine Philips did not write to be published but her work was being circulated before 1651. Born in London, at 16 she married a man 38 years older than her and moved to Wales. She was known as 'the matchless Orinda' and had Royalist sympathies, even though her husband was a member of Cromwell's Parliament.

Edgar Allan Poe (1809–49). Born in Boston to parents who were both actors, Edgar Allan Poe was forced to enlist in the army when he ran up gambling debts. Failing as a soldier, he embarked upon a literary career. He won prizes and was widely published but earned little. He struggled throughout his life with mental instability and succumbed eventually to alcohol poisoning.

Alexander Pushkin (1799–1837). Alexander Pushkin is recognized as the greatest Russian poet, pioneering the use of the vernacular in his work – poetry and drama. Born in Moscow, he was already a literary figure by the time he left school. A champion of liberal views, his most famous play *Boris Godunov*, was written in exile, not being published until many years later. His verse novel, *Eugene Onegin*, was published episodically from 1825 until 1832. He died after challenging his wife's lover to a duel.

Sir Walter Raleigh (*c.*1552–1618). Born in Devon, Sir Walter Raleigh was educated at Oriel College, Oxford. He became a favourite of Queen Elizabeth I and many of his poems were written in praise of her. He directed the colonization of Virginia and introduced tobacco from the colony to England. After Elizabeth's death, he spent many of his later years in prison eventually being executed for alleged treason.

Christina Rossetti (1830–94). Sister of the Pre-Raphaelite painter and poet, Dante Gabriel Rossetti, for most of her life Christina Rossetti lived with her mother. She published her first poems under a pseudonym and her first collection, *Goblin Market and Other Poems*, was published in 1866.

Dante Gabriel Rossetti (1828–82). Dante Gabriel Rossetti studied at a number of art schools before forming the brief but influential Pre-Raphaelite Brotherhood with some other painters, critics and writers, with the aim of taking art back to the quattrocento. In the 1850s, he moved towards aestheticism. *The House of Love*, 102 sonnets written between 1847 and 1881, is recognized as Rossetti's poetic masterpiece.

Sir Walter Scott (1771–1832). Born in Edinburgh, Sir Walter Scott was the first English language author to have a truly international career. His books – including such classics as *Waverley, Ivanhoe, Rob Roy*, and *The Heart of Midlothian* – were read in Europe, Australia and America. His poetry, including the popular *The Lady in the Lake* brought him considerable fame.

William Shakespeare (1564–1616). Ironically, although Shakespeare is the greatest of all English writers, comparatively little is known about his life. Born in Stratford, his father a glove-maker, his mother the daughter of a rich farmer, he received no university education. He moved to London in the early 1590s, married Anne Hathaway and was for most of his life an actor, playwright and principal shareholder of the most successful theatrical company in England.

Percy Bysshe Shelley (1792–1822). Born near Horsham in Surrey, Percy Bysshe Shelley was sent down from Oxford for atheism. In London he came under the influence of the social philosopher William Godwin, falling in love with Godwin's daughter, Mary, later author of *Frankenstein*, before eloping to Europe with her. Shelley drowned in a squall in the Gulf of Spezia, aged 30.

Sir Philip Sidney (1554–86). Born into a family of poets in Kent, Sir Philip Sidney's father had been Lord Deputy of Ireland. He studied at both Oxford and Cambridge, after which he travelled in Europe. Ostracized from court when he criticized the possibility of Queen Elizabeth marrying a Catholic, he used his banishment to write poetry. He was made Governor of Flushing, an English possession in the Low Countries in 1586 and died from a wound in the leg, gained in battle, aged 32.

Edmund Spenser (*c.*1552–99). After studying as a 'poor scholar' at Cambridge, Spenser gained employment working as secretary to several prominent men. He went to Ireland as secretary to the Lord Governor, remaining there as a civil servant, settler and landowner for the rest of his life. The royal recognition he hoped for, especially after publishing his epic, *The Faerie Queene*, never arrived.

Robert Louis Stevenson (1850–94). Novelist, poet and travel writer, Robert Louis Stevenson was born into a famous family of lighthouse designers. He was first published at 16 but was expected to become an engineer. However, he decided on becoming a writer, studying law as a compromise although he never practised. Amongst his much-loved novels are *Kidnapped* and *The Strange Case of Dr. Jekyll and Mr. Hyde*.

William Strode (1598–1645). William Strode was born in Devon and educated at Westminster School and Oxford where he began to write poetry. He entered the clergy, becoming chaplain to the Bishop of Oxford. Although an eminent poet of his time, his work was forgotten until the early 20th century.

Sir John Suckling (1609–42). Born into an old Norfolk family and educated at Cambridge, the 'Cavalier' poet and playwright Sir John Suckling was one of the most ardent gamblers of his time. He took part in an embassy to Germany in 1631 and fought on the losing Royalist side against the Scots in 1639. When his plot to free the imprisoned Earl of Stafford was uncovered in 1641, he was forced to flee to France where he took poison and killed himself.

Alfred, Lord Tennyson (1809–92). Tennyson began to write while still a child as an escape from his drunken and violent father. Born in Lincolnshire, he was educated at Cambridge and published some of his best-loved poems at the age of 20. His work was often dominated by the melancholia with which he was plagued throughout his life, but his poems achieved great popularity.

Edward Thomas (1878–1917). Edward Thomas was born in London and educated at Oxford. He was forced to write prolifically in order to support his family. In 1914 he started to write poetry, encouraged by his friend, the poet Robert Frost. Enlisting in the army in 1915, he was killed at Arris two years later.

Herbert Trench (1865–1923). Irish poet Herbert Trench was born in Avonmore, County Cork and educated at Oxford. He worked as an examiner for the Board of Education from 1891. His poem *Apollo and the Seaman* was turned into an opera by Joseph Holbrooke and performed with Thomas Beecham as conductor. Following this, Trench moved into theatrical work before spending time travelling. He died in Boulogne-sur-Mer.

Edmund Waller (1607–87). Born into a wealthy Hertfordshire family, Edmund Waller became an MP at 16. He switched sides in the Civil War from Parliamentarian to Royalist and narrowly avoided execution in 1643 for taking part in a Royalist plot. Sent into exile, he travelled in France, Italy and Switzerland, returning to Parliament after the Restoration.

Walt Whitman (1819–92). Born on Long Island and brought up in Brooklyn, New York, Walt Whitman left school at 11 and worked in a number of jobs before establishing a career as a journalist. After the American Civil War, he worked at the Department of the Interior but was fired in 1855 when his book *Leaves of Grass* was published. It was seen as scandalous but it was his masterpiece, taking what he described as 'the United States themselves' as his subject.

John Wilbye (1574–1638). Madrigal composer John Wilbye was born near Diss in Suffolk, the son of a tanner. He is the greatest of all English madrigalists, his pieces appearing to this day in modern collections.

Oscar Wilde (1854–1900). Playwright, poet, novelist and short story-writer, Oscar Wilde was one of the most successful playwrights of the late Victorian period with plays such as *The Importance of Being Earnest*, a smash hit of the time. In 1895, he was sentenced to two years' hard labour after being convicted of 'gross indecency' with other men. On his release he sailed for France where he died.

William Wordsworth (1770–1850). Born in Cockermouth in the Lake District of England, William Wordsworth was educated at Cambridge. During a walking tour of Europe in his early twenties, he came into contact with the ideals of the French Revolution. He settled in the Lake District with his sister Dorothy, and remained there for most of his life. In 1798, with the poet Samuel Taylor Coleridge, he published *Lyrical Ballads*, one of the most important books of poetry in the history of English literature.

Sir Thomas Wyatt (1503–42). Sir Thomas Wyatt was born at Allingham Castle in Kent and occupied various positions at court. Knighted in 1535, he was imprisoned several times for brawling and possibly also for sexual misconduct after separating from his wife. In 1541 he was accused of treason and in 1544 his son was hanged on the same charge. As a translator of Petrarch, Wyatt introduced the sonnet form to English literature.

Index of First Lines

Index of Poets

Index of Poems